The Best Harrison Ford Characters, Including Indiana Jones, Han Solo, Jack Ryan and More

Victoria Hockfield

The role of the book within our culture is changing. The change is brought on by new ways to acquire & use content, the rapid dissemination of information and real-time peer collaboration on a global scale. Despite these changes one thing is clear--"the book" in it's traditional form continues to play an important role in learning and communication. The book you are holding in your hands utilizes the unique characteristics of the Internet -- relying on web infrastructure and collaborative tools to share and use resources in keeping with the characteristics of the medium (user-created, defying control, etc.)--while maintaining all the convenience and utility of a real book.

Contents

Articles

References

Indiana Jones

Indiana Jones

Indiana Jones character	
Harrison Ford as Indiana Jones in *Indiana Jones and the Raiders of the Lost Ark*	
First appearance	*Indiana Jones and the Raiders of the Lost Ark*
Last appearance	*Indiana Jones and the Kingdom of the Crystal Skull*
Created by	George Lucas
Portrayed by	**Films:** Harrison Ford (ages 36–58) River Phoenix (age 13) **TV series:** Neil Boulane (baby) Corey Carrier (ages 8–10) Sean Patrick Flanery (ages 16–21) George Hall (age 93) **Video games:** Doug Lee (voice) David Esch (voice)
Nickname(s)	Indiana Indy Junior
Occupation	Archaeologist Associate dean College professor Soldier Spy
Title	Doctor
Family	Henry Walton Jones, Sr. (father, deceased) Anna Mary Jones (mother, deceased)
Spouse(s)	Deirdre Campbell Jones(1926) Marion Ravenwood Jones(1957-?)

Children	Henry Walton Jones III A daughter (name unrevealed)
Relatives	Susie Jones (sister, deceased) Pete (uncle, surname unrevealed) Fred (uncle, surname unrevealed) Grace (aunt, surname unrevealed) Frank (cousin, surname unrevealed) Caroline (granddaughter) Spike (grandson) Lucy (granddaughter) Annie Jones (great-granddaughter) Harry Jones (great-grandson)
Religion	Christian/Agnostic
Nationality	American

Dr. Henry Walton "Indiana" Jones, Jr. Ph.D. is a fictional American adventurer, OSS operative, professor of archaeology, and the central protagonist of the *Indiana Jones* franchise. George Lucas created the character in homage to the action heroes of 1930s film serials. The character first appeared in the 1981 film *Raiders of the Lost Ark*, to be followed by *Indiana Jones and the Temple of Doom* in 1984, *Indiana Jones and the Last Crusade* in 1989, *The Young Indiana Jones Chronicles* from 1992 to 1996, and *Kingdom of the Crystal Skull* in 2008. Alongside the more widely known films and television programs, novels, comics, video games, and other media also feature the character, Jones is also featured in the theme park attraction Indiana Jones Adventure, which exists in similar forms at Disneyland and Tokyo DisneySea.

Jones is most famously played by Harrison Ford and has also been portrayed by River Phoenix (as the young Jones in *The Last Crusade*), and in the television series *The Young Indiana Jones Chronicles* by Corey Carrier, Sean Patrick Flanery, and George Hall. Doug Lee has supplied Jones's voice to two LucasArts video games, *Indiana Jones and the Fate of Atlantis* and *Indiana Jones and the Infernal Machine*, while David Esch supplied his voice to *Indiana Jones and the Emperor's Tomb.*

Particularly notable facets of the character include his iconic look (bullwhip, fedora, and leather jacket), sense of humor, deep knowledge of many ancient civilizations and languages, and fear of snakes.

Indiana Jones remains one of cinema's most revered movie characters. In 2003, he was ranked as the second greatest movie hero of all time by the American Film Institute. He was also named the sixth greatest movie character by *Empire* magazine. *Entertainment Weekly* ranked Indy 2nd on their list of *The All-Time Coolest Heroes in Pop Culture*. *Premiere* magazine also placed Indy at number 7 on their list of *The 100 Greatest Movie Characters of All Time.* Since his first appearance in *Raiders of the Lost Ark*, he has become a worldwide star. On their list of the *100 Greatest Fictional Characters*,

Fandomania.com ranked Indy at number 10. In 2010, he ranked #2 on *Time* Magazine's list of the greatest fictional characters of all time, surpassed only by Sherlock Holmes.

Appearances

Indiana Jones, played by Harrison Ford, was first introduced in the 1981 film *Raiders of the Lost Ark*, set in 1936. He is portrayed as an adventurous throwback to the 1930s film serial treasure hunters and pulp action heroes, with an alter ego of Doctor Jones, a respected archaeology professor at Marshall College (named after producer Frank Marshall) a fictional college in Connecticut. In this first adventure, he is pitted against the Nazis, traveling the world to prevent them from recovering the Ark of the Covenant (see also Biblical archaeology). He is aided by Marion Ravenwood and Sallah. The Nazis are led by Jones's archrival, a Nazi-sympathizing French archaeologist named René Belloq, and Arnold Toht, a sinister Gestapo agent.

The 1984 prequel, *Indiana Jones and the Temple of Doom*, set in 1935, took the character into a more horror-oriented story, skipping his legitimate teaching job and globe trotting, and taking place almost entirely in India. This time, Jones attempts to recover children and the Sankara stones from the bloodthirsty Thuggee cult. He is aided by Short Round and accompanied by Willy.

The third film, 1989's *Indiana Jones and the Last Crusade*, set in 1938, returned to the formula of the original, reintroducing characters such as Sallah and Marcus Brody, a scene from Professor Jones's classroom (he now teaches at Barnett College), the globe trotting element of multiple locations, and the return of the infamous Nazi mystics, this time trying to find the Holy Grail. The film's introduction, set in 1912, provided some back story to the character, specifically the origin of his fear of snakes, his use of a bullwhip, the scar on his chin, and his hat; the film's epilogue also reveals that "Indiana" is not Jones's first name, but a nickname he took from the family dog. The film was a buddy movie of sorts, teaming Jones with his father, often to comical effect. Although Lucas intended at the time to do five films, this ended up being the last for over eighteen years, as Lucas could not think of a good plot element to drive the next installment.

The 2008 film, *Indiana Jones and the Kingdom of the Crystal Skull*, became the latest film in the series. Set in 1957, 19 years after the third film, it pits an older, wiser Indiana Jones against Soviet agents bent on harnessing the power of a crystal skull discovered in South America by his former colleague Harold Oxley (John Hurt). He is aided in his adventure by an old lover, Marion Ravenwood (Karen Allen), and her son—a young greaser named Mutt Williams (Shia LaBeouf), later revealed to be his biological child Henry Jones III. There are rumors that LaBeouf will take over the Indy franchise. [*citation needed*] This film also reveals that Jones was recruited by the Office of Strategic Services (a predecessor department to the CIA) during World War II, attaining the rank of Colonel and running covert operations with MI6 agent George McHale on the Soviet Union.

Television

From 1992 to 1996, George Lucas executive produced a television series named *The Young Indiana Jones Chronicles*, which was designed as an educational program for children, spotlighting historical figures and important events, using the concept of a prequel to the films as a draw. The show featured a standard formula of a 93-year-old Jones (George Hall), wearing an eye patch, introducing a story, and then an adventure with either a 17-year-old Jones (Sean Patrick Flanery) or a 10-year-old Jones (Corey Carrier), and even a baby Indy (Neil Boulane). Historical figures featured on the show include Mustafa Kemal Atatürk, Leo Tolstoy, Pancho Villa, Charles de Gaulle, Elliot Ness, Ernest Hemingway, Patrick Pearse, Vladimir Lenin, T. E. Lawrence, Winston Churchill, Herman Göring, Theodore Roosevelt, and John Ford, in such diverse locations as Egypt, Austria-Hungary, India, China, and the whole of Europe.

One episode, "Young Indiana Jones and the Mystery of the Blues", is bookended by Harrison Ford, reprising his role as the character. Indiana loses one of his eyes sometime between 1957 and when the "Old Indy" segments take place.

The show provided some backstory for the films, as well as new information regarding the character. He was born July 1, 1899, and his middle name is Walton (Lucas's middle name). It is also mentioned that he had a sister called Suzie who died as an infant of fever, and that he eventually has a daughter and grandchildren who appear in some episode introductions and epilogues. His relationship with his father, first introduced in *Indiana Jones and the Last Crusade*, was further fleshed out with stories about his travels with his father as a young boy. A large portion of the series centered around his activities during World War I.

In 1999, Lucas removed the episode introductions and epilogues by George Hall for the VHS and DVD releases, as he re-edited the episodes into chronologically ordered feature-length stories. The series title was also changed to *The Adventures of Young Indiana Jones*.

In 2008's *Indiana Jones and the Kingdom of the Crystal Skull* film, Jones makes passing mention to the events of the episode in which he met Pancho Villa; this was included to reinforce that the TV series is indeed part of the same official continuity as the movies.

Video games

The character has appeared in several officially licensed video games, beginning with adaptations of *Raiders of the Lost Ark*, *Temple of Doom*, two adaptations of *The Last Crusade* (one with purely action mechanics, one with an adventure and puzzle based structure) and Indiana Jones' Greatest Adventures which included the storylines from all three of the original films.

Following this, the games branched off into original story-lines with Indiana Jones in the Lost Kingdom, *Indiana Jones and the Fate of Atlantis*, *Indiana Jones and the Infernal Machine*, *Indiana Jones and the Emperor's Tomb* and *Indiana Jones and the Staff of Kings*. *Emperor's Tomb* sets up Jones's companion Wu Han and the search for Nurhaci's ashes seen at the beginning of *Temple of*

Doom. The first two games were developed by Hal Barwood and starred Doug Lee as the voice of Indiana Jones; *Emperor's Tomb* had David Esch fill the role and *Staff of Kings* starred John Armstrong.

There is also a small game from Lucas Arts *Indiana Jones and His Desktop Adventures*. A video game was made for young Indy called *Young Indiana Jones and the Instruments of Chaos*, as well as a video game version of *The Young Indiana Jones Chronicles*.

Two Lego Indiana Jones games have also been released. *Lego Indiana Jones: The Original Adventures* was released in 2008 and follows the plots of the first three films. It was followed by *LEGO Indiana Jones 2: The Adventure Continues* in late 2009. The sequel includes an abbreviated reprise of the first three films, but focuses on the plot of *Indiana Jones and the Kingdom of the Crystal Skull*.

Indiana Jones has also made cameo appearances as an unlockable character in the games *Mercenaries: Playground of Destruction* and *Lego Star Wars: The Complete Saga*.

Theme parks

Main article: Indiana Jones Adventure

The Indiana Jones Adventure attractions at Disneyland and Tokyo DisneySea ("Temple of the Forbidden Eye" and "Temple of the Crystal Skull," respectively) place Indy at the forefront of two similar archaeological discoveries. These two temples each contain a wrathful deity who threatens the guests who ride through in World War II troop transports. The attractions, some of the most expensive of their kind at the time, opened in 1995 and 2001, respectively, with sole design credit attributed to Walt Disney Imagineering. Disney did not license Harrison Ford's likeness for the North American version; nevertheless, a differentiated Indiana Jones audio-animatronic character appears at three points in both attractions. However, the Indiana Jones featured in the DisneySea version does use Harrison Ford's likeness but uses Japanese audio for all of his speaking parts.

Disneyland Resort Paris also features an Indiana Jones-titled ride where people speed off through ancient ruins in a runaway mine wagon similar to that found in *Indiana Jones and the Temple of Doom*. *Indiana Jones and the Temple of Peril* is a looping roller coaster engineered by Intamin AG and opened in 1993.

The Indiana Jones Epic Stunt Spectacular! is a live show that has been presented in the Disney's Hollywood Studios theme park of the Walt Disney World Resort with few changes since the park's 1989 opening under a different name. The 25-minute show presents various stunts framed in the context of a feature film production, and recruits members of the audience to participate in the show. Stunt artists in the show re-create and ultimately reveal some of the secrets of the stunts of the *Raiders of the Lost Ark* films, including the well-known "running-from-the-boulder" scene. Stunt performer Anislav Varbanov was fatally injured in August, 2009 while rehearsing the popular show.[citation needed]

Characterization

In his role as a college professor of archaeology, Henry Jones Jr. is scholarly and learned in a tweed suit, lecturing on ancient civilizations. But at the opportunity to recover important artifacts, he transforms into "Indiana," a near superhero image he has concocted for himself. Producer Frank Marshall said, "Indy [is] a fallible character. He makes mistakes and gets hurt. [...] That's the other thing people like: He's a real character, not a character with superpowers." Spielberg said there "was the willingness to allow our leading man to get hurt and to express his pain and to get his mad out and to take pratfalls and sometimes be the butt of his own jokes. I mean, Indiana Jones is not a perfect hero, and his imperfections, I think, make the audience feel that, with a little more exercise and a little more courage, they could be just like him." According to Spielberg biographer Douglas Brode, Indiana created his heroic figure so to escape the dullness of teaching at a school. Both of Indiana's personas reject one another in philosophy, creating a duality. Harrison Ford said the fun of playing the character was because Indiana is both a romantic and a cynic, while scholars have analyzed Indiana as having traits of a lone wolf; a man on a quest; a noble treasure hunter; a hardboiled detective; a human superhero; and an American patriot.

Like many characters in his films, Jones has some autobiographical elements of Spielberg. Indiana lacks a proper father figure because of his strained relationship with his father, Henry Senior. His own contained anger is misdirected at the likes of Professor Abner Ravenwood, his mentor at the University of Chicago, leading to a strained relationship with Marion Ravenwood. The teenage Indiana bases his own look on a figure from the prologue of *Indiana Jones and the Last Crusade*, after being given his hat. Marcus Brody acts as Indiana's positive role model at the college. Indiana's own insecurities are made worse by the absence of his mother. In *Indiana Jones and the Temple of Doom*, the character becomes the father in a temporary family unit with Willie Scott and Short Round to survive. Indiana is rescued from the evil of Kali by Short Round's dedication. Indiana also saves many children from slavery.

Because of Indiana's strained relationship with his father, who was absent much of Indiana's youth searching for the Holy Grail, the character does not pursue the more spiritual aspects of the cultures he studies. Indiana uses his knowledge of Shiva to ultimately defeat Mola Ram. In *Raiders*, however, he is wise enough to close his eyes in the presence of God in the Ark of the Covenant. By contrast, his rival Rene Belloq dies horribly for having the audacity to try to communicate directly with God.

In *Crusade*'s prologue, Indiana's intentions are revealed as prosocial, as he believes artifacts "belong in a museum." In the film's climax, Indiana undergoes "literal" tests of faith to retrieve the Grail and save his father's life. He also remembers Jesus as a historical figure - a humble carpenter - rather than an exalted figure when he recognizes the simple nature and tarnished appearance of the real Grail amongst a large assortment of much more ornately decorated ones. Henry Senior rescues his son from falling to his death when reaching for the fallen Grail, telling him to "let it go," overcoming his mercenary nature. *The Young Indiana Jones Chronicles* explains how Indiana becomes solitary and less idealistic after fighting in World War I. In *Indiana Jones and the Kingdom of the Crystal Skull*, Jones is older and wiser, whereas his sidekicks Mutt and Mac are youthfully arrogant and greedy, respectively.

Concept and creation

Indiana Jones is modeled after the strong-jawed heroes of the matinée serials and pulp magazines that George Lucas and Steven Spielberg enjoyed in their childhoods (such as the Republic Pictures serials, and the Doc Savage series). H. Rider Haggard's adventure hero Alan Quatermain of *King Solomon's Mines* was a notable template for Jones. The two friends first discussed the project in Hawaii around the time of the release of the first *Star Wars* film. Spielberg told Lucas how he wanted his next project to be something fun, like perhaps a James Bond film. According to sources, Lucas responded to the effect that he had something "even better," or that he "got that beat."

The character was originally named "Indiana Smith" (perhaps in a nod to the 1966 Western film *Nevada Smith*), after an Alaskan Malamute Lucas owned in the 1970s ("Indiana"); however, Spielberg disliked the name "Smith," and Lucas casually suggested "Jones" as an alternative.

Wardrobe and equipment

Indiana Jones was designed by comic book artist Jim Steranko. George Lucas suggested the flight jacket (which reminded Steranko of Lucas), the fedora (which reminded him of Humphrey Bogart in *The Treasure of the Sierra Madre*) and a whip (reminiscent of Zorro). Steranko added the Sam Browne belt, a belt with a holster, and the khaki shirt and trousers. Costume designer Deborah Nadoolman Landis said the inspiration for Indiana's outfit was Charlton Heston's Harry Steele in *Secret of the Incas*: "We did watch this film together as a crew several times, and I always thought it strange that the filmmakers did not credit it later as the inspiration for the series."

Upon requests by Spielberg and Lucas, the costume designer gave the character a distinctive silhouette through the styling of the hat; after examining many hats, the designers chose a tall-crowned, wide-brimmed fedora. As a documentary of *Raiders* pointed out, the hat served a practical purpose. Following the lead of the old "B"-movies that inspired the *Indiana Jones* series, the fedora hid the actor's face sufficiently to allow doubles to perform the more dangerous stunts seamlessly. Examples in *Raiders* include the wider-angle shot of Indy and Marion crashing a statue through a wall, and Indy sliding under a fast-moving vehicle from front to back. Thus it was necessary for the hat to stay in place much of the time.

The hat became so iconic that the filmmakers could only come up with very good reasons or jokes to remove it. If it ever fell off during a take, filming would have to stop to put it back on. In jest, Ford put a stapler against his head when a documentary crew visited during shooting of *The Last Crusade*. This created the urban legend that Ford stapled the hat to his head. Although other hats were also used throughout the movies, the general style and profile remained the same. Elements of the outfit include:

- The fedora was supplied by Herbert Johnson Hatters in England for the first three films. It was referred to as "The Australian Model" by costume designer Deborah Nadoolman Landis and was fitted with a Petersham bow. Indy's fedora for *Crystal Skull* were made by Steve Delk and Marc Kitter of the Adventurebilt Hat Company.
- The leather jacket, a hybrid of the "Type 440" and the A-2 jacket, were made by Leather Concessionaires (now known as Wested Leather Co). *Raiders of the Lost Ark* and *The Last Crusade*. For *Temple of Doom*, jackets were made in house at Bermans & Nathans in London based on a stunt jacket they provided for Raiders of The Lost Ark, while Tony Nowak made the jacket in *Kingdom of the Crystal Skull*.
- The bag was a modified Mark VII British gas mask bag.
- The whip was a 8 to 10 foot (2.4 to 3.0 m) bullwhip crafted by David Morgan for the first three films. The whips for *Crystal Skull* were crafted by a variety of people, including Terry Jacka, Joe Strain and Morgan (different lengths and styles were likely used in specific stunts).
- The pistol was usually a World War I-era revolver, including the Webley Green (*Last Crusade* and *Crystal Skull*), or a .45 ACP Smith & Wesson Hand Ejector 2nd model revolver (*Raiders*). He has also used an M1917 revolver (*Temple of Doom*), a Nagant M1895 (*Young Indiana Jones*), and a 9 mm Browning Hi-Power (*Raiders*).
- The shoes were "Indy Boots" made by Alden Shoes, still sold today (though in a redder (brick) shade of brown than seen in the movies).

Jones's fedora and leather jacket (as used in *The Last Crusade*) are on display at the Smithsonian's American History Museum in Washington, D.C. The collection of props and clothing from the films has become a thriving hobby for some aficionados of the franchise. Jones' whip was the third most popular film weapon, as shown by a 2008 poll held by 20th Century Fox, which surveyed approximately two thousand film fans.

Casting

Originally, Spielberg suggested Harrison Ford; Lucas resisted the idea, since he had already cast the actor in three of his movies (*American Graffiti*, *Star Wars*, and *The Empire Strikes Back*), and did not want Ford to become known as his "Bobby De Niro" (in reference to the fact that fellow director Martin Scorsese regularly cast Robert De Niro in his films). During an intensive casting process, Lucas and Spielberg auditioned many actors, and finally cast then little-known actor Tom Selleck as Indiana Jones. Shortly afterward pre-production began in earnest on *Raiders of the Lost Ark*.

However, CBS refused to release Selleck from his contractual commitment to *Magnum, P.I.* (which was gradually gaining momentum in the ratings), forcing him to turn down the role. After Spielberg suggested Ford again, Lucas finally gave in, and he was cast in the role — less than 3 weeks before filming of *Raiders* began.

One of CBS's concerns was that shooting for *Magnum P.I.* conflicted with shooting for *Raiders*, both of which were to begin about the same time. However, Selleck was to say later in an interview that shooting for *Magnum P.I.* was delayed and did not actually begin until shooting for *Raiders* had concluded. Sadly for Selleck, he could have finished his participation in *Raiders* and still had time to return for *Magnum*.

Models

Many people are said to be the real-life inspiration of the Indiana Jones character — although none of the following have been confirmed as inspirations by Lucas or Spielberg. In alphabetical order by last name:

- Beloit College professor and paleontologist Roy Chapman Andrews.
- Italian archaeologist and circus strongman Giovanni Battista Belzoni (1778–1823).
- Yale University professor, historian, and explorer Hiram Bingham III, who rediscovered and excavated the lost city of Machu Picchu, and chronicled his find in the bestselling book *The Lost City of the Incas* in 1948.
- The University of Chicago archaeologist Robert Braidwood.
- Fellow University of Chicago archaeologist James Henry Breasted.
- The British archaeologist Percy Fawcett, who spent much of his life exploring the jungles of northern Brazil, and who was last seen in 1925 returning to the Amazon Basin to look for the Lost City Of Z. A fictionalized version of Fawcett appears to Jones in the book *Indiana Jones And The Seven Veils*.
- British archaeologist and soldier T. E. Lawrence.
- William Montgomery McGovern.
- Frederick Albert Mitchell-Hedges.
- German archaeologist Otto Rahn.

George Lucas has said on various occasions that Sean Connery's portrayal of British secret agent James Bond was one of the primary inspirations for Jones, a reason Connery was chosen for the role of Indiana's father in the third film, *Indiana Jones and the Last Crusade*.

Influence

Though some archaeologists criticize Indy's methods as befitting a "looter" rather more than a careful worker of precious sites, many have adopted the popular figure as something of a standard-bearer for their profession. The industry magazine *Archaeology*, believing that Jones, as one editor said, was "a horrible archaeologist but a great diplomat for archeology," named eight past and current archaeologists who they felt "embodied [Jones'] spirit" as recipients of the "Indy Spirit Awards" in 2008. That same year Ford himself was elected to the Board of Directors of the Archaeological Institute of America. Commenting that "understanding the past can only help us in dealing with the present and the future,"

Ford was praised by the association's president for his character's "significant role in stimulating the public's interest in archaeological exploration."

While himself a homage to various prior adventurers, aspects of Indiana Jones also directly influenced some subsequent characterizations:

- Lara Croft, the female archaeologist of the *Tomb Raider* franchise, was originally designed as a man, but was changed to a woman, partly because the developers felt that the original design was too similar to Indiana Jones. Paramount Pictures, which distributed the Indiana Jones film series, would later make two films based on the *Tomb Raider* games.
- *Prince of Persia* producer Ben Mattes explained that their "inspiration was anything Harrison Ford has ever done: Indiana Jones, Han Solo."
- The video game series *Uncharted* is also very heavily influenced by Indiana Jones, as well as some of the influences that led to Indiana Jones himself, such as pulp magazines and movie serials. The design team felt the sources shared themes of mystery and "what-if scenarios" that romanticized adventure and aimed to include those in *Uncharted*.
- Jack West Jr, a character featured in 3 Matthew Reilly books, (*Seven Ancient Wonders*, *The Six Sacred Stones* and *The Five Greatest Warriors*) is heavily influenced by Indiana Jones. Reilly himself is a big fan of George Lucas.
- Ben Franklin Gates of the National Treasure series.

External links

- IndianaJones.com [1] — the official Indiana Jones site
- Indiana Jones [2] at the Internet Movie Database

Indiana Jones (franchise)

Indiana Jones franchise	
Creator	George Lucas
Original work	*Raiders of the Lost Ark*
Print publications	
Books	See the Literature section
Novels	See the Adult novels section
Comics	Indiana Jones comic books
Films and television	
Films	*Raiders of the Lost Ark* *Temple of Doom* *The Last Crusade* *Kingdom of the Crystal Skull*
Television series	*The Young Indiana Jones Chronicles*
Games	
Traditional	See the Merchandise section
Role-playing	*Indiana Jones* role-playing game
Video games	See the Merchandise section
Audio	
Soundtracks	*Raiders of the Lost Ark*, *Temple of Doom*, *The Last Crusade*, *Kingdom of the Crystal Skull*
Miscellaneous	
Toys	See the Toy lines section, Lego Indiana Jones

The ***Indiana Jones* franchise**, based on the historical fantasy adventures of the eponymous fictional archaeologist, began in 1981 with the film *Raiders of the Lost Ark*. A prequel, *Indiana Jones and the Temple of Doom*, followed in 1984 and the sequel *Indiana Jones and the Last Crusade* in 1989. In 1992, *The Young Indiana Jones Chronicles* began airing on television. A fourth film, *Indiana Jones and the Kingdom of the Crystal Skull*, was released on May 22, 2008. The series was created by George Lucas; the films star Harrison Ford and were directed by Steven Spielberg.

In addition, Marvel Comics began publishing *The Further Adventures of Indiana Jones* in 1983, and Dark Horse Comics earned the comic book rights to the character in 1991. Novelizations of the films have been published, in addition to a series of German novels by Wolfgang Hohlbein, and twelve novels set before the films published by Bantam Books. Numerous video games about Indiana Jones have been released since 1982.

Films

Overview

Raiders of the Lost Ark (1981) is set in 1936. Indiana Jones (Harrison Ford) is assigned by government agents to locate the Ark of the Covenant before the Nazis do, to make them invincible like the Israelites in the Old Testament, who revered it as the dwelling place of God. The Nazis are being helped by Indiana's nemesis René Belloq (Paul Freeman). With the help of his old flame Marion Ravenwood (Karen Allen) and Sallah (John Rhys-Davies), Indiana manages to recover the Ark in Egypt. The Nazis manage to steal the Ark and capture Indiana and Marion. Belloq and the Nazis perform a ceremony to open the Ark, but when they do so, they are all killed gruesomely by the Ark's wrath. Indiana and Marion, who survived by closing their eyes, manage to get the Ark back to America, where it is stored in a secretive government warehouse.

Indiana Jones and the Temple of Doom (1984) is set in 1935, a year before *Raiders*. Indiana escapes Chinese gangsters with the help of singer/actress Willie Scott (Kate Capshaw) and his eleven-year-old sidekick Short Round (Jonathan Ke Quan). The trio crash-land in India where they come across a village whose children have been kidnapped. A destructive cult led by Mola Ram (Amrish Puri) have also taken the holy Sankara Stones, which they will use to take over the world. Indiana manages to overcome Mola Ram's evil power, and rescues the children and returns the stones to their rightful place, overcoming his own mercenary nature.

Indiana Jones and the Last Crusade (1989) opens in 1912 where a thirteen-year-old Indiana (River Phoenix) attempts to recover an ornamental cross belonging to Francisco Vásquez de Coronado, a task which he finally completes in 1938. Indiana along with his friend Marcus Brody (Denholm Elliott) are assigned by American businessman Walter Donovan (Julian Glover) to find the Holy Grail. They are teamed up with Dr. Elsa Schneider (Alison Doody), following on from where Indiana's estranged father Henry (Sean Connery) left off before he disappeared. It turns out Donovan and Elsa are in league with the Nazis, who captured Henry in order to get Indiana to help them find the Grail. However, Indiana recovers his father's diary filled with his research, and manages to rescue him before finding the location of the Grail. Both Donovan and Elsa fall to the temptation of the Grail, while Indiana and Henry realize that their relationship with each other is more important than finding the relic.

Indiana Jones and the Kingdom of the Crystal Skull (2008) is set in 1957, making it nineteen years since *The Last Crusade*, and thus acknowledging the real-life passing of years between films. Indiana is having a quiet life teaching before being thrust back into his old adventuring. He races against agents of the Soviet Union, led by Irina Spalko (Cate Blanchett) for the Crystal Skull. Indy's journey takes him across Nevada, Connecticut, Peru, and the forest of the Amazon in Brazil. In the film Indiana is faced with betrayal by one of his best friends Mac (Ray Winstone) is introduced to a greaser named Mutt

Williams (Shia LaBeouf), who turns out to be his son, and is reunited with his old flame Marion Ravenwood.

Development

In 1973, George Lucas wrote *The Adventures of Indiana Smith.* Like *Star Wars,* it was an opportunity to create a modern version of the serials of the 1930s and 1940s. Lucas discussed the concept with Philip Kaufman, who worked with him for several weeks and came up with the Ark of the Covenant as the plot device. The project was stalled when Clint Eastwood hired Kaufman to direct *The Outlaw Josey Wales.* In May 1977, Lucas was in Maui, trying to escape the enormous success of *Star Wars.* Friend and colleague Steven Spielberg was also there, holidaying from work on *Close Encounters of the Third Kind.* Spielberg told Lucas he was interested in making a James Bond film. Lucas then told him of an idea "better than James Bond", explaining the plot of *Raiders of the Lost Ark.* Spielberg loved it, calling it "a James Bond film without the hardware", though he had the character's surname changed to "Jones". Spielberg and Lucas made a deal with Paramount Pictures for five films about Indiana.

Spielberg and Lucas aimed to make *Indiana Jones and the Temple of Doom* much darker, because of their personal moods following their respective break-ups and divorces. Lucas made the film a prequel as he didn't want the Nazis to be the villains again. He had ideas regarding the Monkey King and a haunted castle, but wound up creating the Sankara Stones. He hired Willard Huyck and Gloria Katz to write the script as he knew of their interest in Indian culture. The major scenes that were dropped from *Raiders of the Lost Ark* were included in this film: an escape using a giant rolling gong as a shield, a fall out of a plane in a raft, and a mine cart chase. For the third film, Spielberg revisited the Monkey King and haunted castle concepts, before Lucas suggested the Holy Grail. Spielberg had previously rejected it as too ethereal, but then came up with telling a father-son story. He thought, "The Grail that everybody seeks could be a metaphor for a son seeking reconciliation with a father and a father seeking reconciliation with a son."

Following the 1989 release of *Indiana Jones and the Last Crusade*, Lucas let the series end as he felt he could not think of a good plot device to drive the next installment, and chose instead to produce *The Young Indiana Jones Chronicles*, which explored the character in his early years. Ford played Indiana in one episode, narrating his adventures in 1920 Chicago. When Lucas shot Ford's role in December 1992, he realized the scene opened up the possibility of a film with an older Indiana set in the 1950s. The film could reflect a science fiction 1950s B-movie, with aliens as the plot device. Ford disliked the new angle, telling Lucas "No way am I being in a Steve Spielberg movie like that." Spielberg himself, who depicted aliens in *Close Encounters of the Third Kind* and *E.T. the Extra-Terrestrial*, resisted it. Lucas came up with a story, which Jeb Stuart turned into a script from October 1993 to May 1994. Lucas wanted Indiana to get married, which would allow Henry Jones Sr. to return, expressing concern over whether his son is happy with what he has accomplished. After he learned that Joseph Stalin was interested in psychic warfare, he decided to have Russians as the villains and the aliens to have psychic powers. Following Stuart's next draft, Lucas hired *Last Crusade* writer Jeffrey Boam to write the next three versions, the last of which was completed in March 1996. Three months later, *Independence Day* was released, and Spielberg told Lucas he would not make another alien invasion film. Lucas decided to focus on the *Star Wars* prequels.

In 2000, Spielberg's son asked when the next *Indiana Jones* film would be released, which made him interested in reviving the project. The same year, Ford, Lucas, Spielberg, Frank Marshall, and Kathleen Kennedy met during the American Film Institute's tribute to Ford, and decided they wanted to enjoy the experience of making an Indiana Jones film again. Spielberg also found returning to the series a respite from his many dark films during this period. Spielberg and Lucas discussed the central idea of a B-movie involving aliens, and Lucas suggested using the crystal skulls to ground the idea. Lucas found those artifacts as fascinating as the Ark, and had intended to feature them for a *Young Indiana Jones* episode before the show's cancellation. M. Night Shyamalan was hired to write for an intended 2002 shoot, but he was overwhelmed writing a sequel to a film he loved like *Raiders*, and claimed it was difficult to get Ford, Spielberg, and Lucas to focus. Stephen Gaghan and Tom Stoppard were also approached.

Frank Darabont, who wrote various *Young Indiana Jones* episodes, was hired to write in May 2002. His script, entitled *Indiana Jones and the City of Gods*, was set in the 1950s, with ex-Nazis pursuing Jones. Spielberg conceived the idea because of real life figures such as Juan Perón in Argentina, who protected Nazi war criminals. Darabont claimed Spielberg loved the script, but Lucas had issues with it, and decided to take over writing himself. Lucas and Spielberg acknowledged the 1950s setting could not ignore the Cold War, and the Russians were more plausible villains. Spielberg decided he could not satirize the Nazis after directing *Schindler's List*, while Ford felt "We plum[b] wore the Nazis out." Darabont's main contribution was reintroducing Marion Ravenwood as Indiana's love interest, but gave them a 13-year old daughter, which Spielberg decided was too similar to *The Lost World: Jurassic Park*.

Jeff Nathanson met with Spielberg and Lucas in August 2004, and turned in the next drafts in October and November 2005, titled *The Atomic Ants*. David Koepp continued on from there, giving his script the subtitle *Destroyer of Worlds*, based on the Robert Oppenheimer quote. It was changed to *Kingdom of the Crystal Skull*, as Spielberg found it more inviting a title and actually named the plot device. Koepp wanted to make Mutt into a nerd, but Lucas refused, explaining he had to resemble Marlon Brando in *The Wild One*; "he needs to be what Indiana Jones' father thought of [him] – the curse returns in the form of his own son – he's everything a father can't stand". Koepp collaborated with Lawrence Kasdan on the film's "love dialogue".

Future

The introduction of Mutt Williams (Shia LaBeouf) in *Kingdom of the Crystal Skull* has led to speculation that he will take over the franchise from Ford. In an interview with *IGN*, "Spielberg indicated that LaBeouf has to make multiple *Transformers* movies before he can move over and take on the fedora and bullwhip of Indiana Jones." The actor himself said, "Am I into it? Who wouldn't be? I don't think that's reality. It's a fun rumor." Ford said he would return for a fifth film if it doesn't take another twenty years to develop, while Spielberg responded it would happen "only if you [the audience] want more".

George Lucas made another suggestion that there would be a fifth film. While at the 2008 Cannes Film Festival, he revealed his idea "to make Shia LaBeouf the lead character next time and have Harrison Ford come back like Sean Connery did in the third film". Lucas has also said that age will not be a factor, as Ford was "65 and did everything in *Crystal Skull*. The old chemistry is there, and it's not like he's an old man. He's incredibly agile; he looks even better than he did 20 years ago, if you ask me". In August 2008, Lucas was researching potential plot devices, and stated Spielberg was more open to the idea of the fifth film. He also changed his mind about continuing the series with a spin-off, joking "Indiana Jones is Indiana Jones. Harrison Ford is Indiana Jones. If it was Mutt Williams it would be *Mutt Williams and the Search for Elvis* or something." Two months later, Ford stated that he would not return if the fifth film was an animated film like *The Clone Wars*, because "I'd hate to see it reduced in any way from the movies that we have done and the way we have done them." He also called Lucas' concept for the fifth film "crazy but great".

When asked how being married to Marion Ravenwood and having a son would affect the character in a fifth film, Ford only replied "He's seen something. Remember those are the only witness to what he's seen. That's kind of interesting."

Speaking to BBC journalist Lizo Mzimba in June 2009, LaBeouf confirmed that "Steven [Spielberg] just said that he cracked the story on it [the fifth film], I think they're gearing that up."

Speaking to Le Figaro on September 14, 2009, Ford said that "the story for the new *Indiana Jones* is in the process of taking form. Steven Spielberg, George Lucas and myself are agreed on what the fifth adventure will concern, and George is actively at work. If the script is good, I'll be very happy to put the costume on again."

In an interview with thearnoldfans.com on December 3, 2009, George Lucas was asked about the status of a new film and replied, "The next Indy film? Yes, we're working on it. It's in development. That's all I can say right now."

In a January 8 interview with MTV, Ford said, "George is working on an idea, and if it comes to a fruitful stage, all of us are very interested in making another...I think it would be interesting to advance the understanding of the character, as we always have had that ambition throughout the series. I think it would be interesting to deepen the relationship between he and his son and play on that relationship. ...

It's full of opportunity. The series is full of opportunity."

In an interview with *Time*, when asked about passing the fedora to Shia in the next Indy movie, Ford said, "What are you talking about? It's mine. I would love to do another Indiana Jones movie. George Lucas is working on an idea now. Shia can get his own hat. I earned that hat."

On June 7, 2010 reports surfaced about a possible *Indiana Jones 5*. It was highly speculated that the fifth installment would start shooting in 2011 and involved a plot that revolved around the Bermuda Triangle. The story was later confirmed as "completely false" by Frank Marshall on his Twitter page.

Reception

Box office performance

Film	Release date	Box office revenue			Box office ranking		Budget	Ref
		North America	Foreign	Worldwide	All time domestic	All time worldwide		
Raiders of the Lost Ark	June 12, 1981 (July 16, 1982)(R) (March 25, 1983)(R)	$242,374,454 (R)	$141,766,000	$384,140,454	#57 #16 (A)	#123	$18,000,000	
Indiana Jones and the Temple of Doom	May 23, 1984	$179,870,271	$153,237,000	$333,107,271	#126 #83 (A)	#178	$28,000,000	
Indiana Jones and the Last Crusade	May 24, 1989	$197,171,806	$277,000,000	$474,171,806	#100 #93 (A)	#80	$48,000,000	
Indiana Jones and the Kingdom of the Crystal Skull	May 22, 2008	$317,101,119	$469,534,914	$786,636,033	#24 #119 (A)	#26	$185,000,000	
Total		$936,517,650	$1,041,537,914	$1,978,055,564			$279,000,000	

List indicator(s)

- (A) indicates the **adjusted totals** based on current ticket prices (calculated by Box Office Mojo).
- (R) totals for the domestic release and the following 2 re-releases of *Raiders of the Lost Ark*.

Critical reaction

Film	Rotten Tomatoes		Metacritic	Yahoo! Movies
	Overall	Cream of the Crop		
Raiders of the Lost Ark	94% (47 reviews)	67% (6 reviews)	90 (11 reviews)	A (7 reviews)
Indiana Jones and the Temple of Doom	84% (58 reviews)	50% (6 reviews)		
Indiana Jones and the Last Crusade	89% (54 reviews)	71% (7 reviews)	65 (14 reviews)	A- (5 reviews)
Indiana Jones and the Kingdom of the Crystal Skull	77% (248 reviews)	59% (39 reviews)	65 (40 reviews)	B (15 reviews)
Average Ratings	**86%**	**62%**	**55**	**N/A**

Academy Awards

Award	Awards Won			
	Raiders of the Lost Ark	***Temple of Doom***	***Last Crusade***	***Kingdom of the Crystal Skull***
Art Direction	Win			
Best Sound	Win		Nomination	
Cinematography	Nomination			
Director	Nomination			
Film Editing	Win			
Music (Original Score)	Nomination	Nomination	Nomination	
Picture	Nomination			
Sound Editing			Win	
Visual Effects	Win	Win		
Special Achievement Award	Win (Ben Burtt and Richard L. Anderson)			

Television

Main article: The Young Indiana Jones Chronicles

A TV series, entitled *The Young Indiana Jones Chronicles*, ran from 1992 to 1996, and featured three incarnations of Indy; Sean Patrick Flanery played Indy aged 16–20; Corey Carrier played the 8-10 Indy in several episodes; and George Hall narrated the show as the 93-year old Indy, who bookended each episode. Lucas began developing the series in 1990 as "edutainment" that would be more cerebral than the films. The show was his first collaboration with producer Rick McCallum, and he wrote the stories for each episode. Writers and directors on the show included Carrie Fisher, Frank Darabont, Vic Armstrong, Ben Burtt, Terry Jones, Nicolas Roeg, Mike Newell and Joe Johnston. In the show, Indy crosses path with many historical figures, who were played by stars such as Daniel Craig, Christopher Lee, Bob Peck, Jeffrey Wright, Marc Warren, Catherine Zeta-Jones, Elizabeth Hurley, Anne Heche, Vanessa Redgrave, Julian Fellowes, Timothy Spall, and even Harrison Ford as the 50-year old Indy in a season two episode (taking the usual place of Hall).

The show was ambitiously shot across over 25 countries for over 150 weeks. Series one shot from March 1991—March 1992, while the second series began two months later and wrapped in April 1993. The American Broadcasting Company were unsure of Lucas's cerebral approach, and attempted to advertise it as an action-adventure like the films. Ratings were decent if unspectacular, and ABC was nervous enough to put it on hiatus after six episodes until September 1992. With only four episodes left of the second season to air, ABC eventually sold the show to Family. They changed the format from 50-minute episodes to 90-minute TV movies. Filming for the final four episodes took place from January 1994—May 1996. *The Young Indiana Jones Chronicles* received mixed reception from fans, although it won 10 Emmy Awards from 23 nominations, and also earned a 1994 Golden Globe nomination for Best Drama series. It was an experimentation ground in digital effects for Lucasfilm.

As detailed in the revised and updated edition of the book *George Lucas: The Creative Impulse* (by Charles Champlin), Lucas has been working for some time on drastically re-editing and restructuring the show for a DVD release. According to a statement by series producer Rick McCallum of Lucasfilm, this work has been 'ramped up' in order for a boxset release to tie in with the theatrical debut of *Kingdom of the Crystal Skull*. Amongst other extras, the discs will include approximately 100 new historical featurettes, now in production. Major structural changes are alleged to have been made to the show, including the complete removal of the 93 year old Jones 'bookend' sections, extensive re-shoots, and removal of complete episodes for better historical continuity.[*citation needed*]

Characters

Main article: List of characters in the Indiana Jones series

This is a list of characters who have appeared in the *Indiana Jones* film franchise.

Character	Film/TV Series				
	Raiders of the Lost Ark	***Temple of Doom***	***The Last Crusade***	***The Young Indiana Jones Chronicles***	***Kingdom of the Crystal Skull***
Indiana Jones	Harrison Ford		Harrison Ford River Phoenix	Sean Patrick Flanery Corey Carrier George Hall Harrison Ford	Harrison Ford
Marcus Brody	Denholm Elliot		Denholm Elliot		*Mentioned Only*
Marion Ravenwood	Karen Allen				Karen Allen
Sallah	John Rhys-Davies		John Rhys-Davies		
Henry Jones, Sr.			Sean Connery Alex Hyde-White	Lloyd Owen	*Mentioned Only*
Toht	Ronald Lacey				
René Belloq	Paul Freeman				
Willie Scott		Kate Capshaw			
Short Round		Jonathan Ke Quan			
Mola Ram		Amrish Puri			
Walter Donovan			Julian Glover		
Elsa Schneider			Alison Doody		
Anna Jones				Ruth de Sosa	
Helen Seymour				Margaret Tyzack	
Remy Baudouin				Ronny Coutteure	
Mac					Ray Winstone
Irina Spalko					Cate Blanchett
Mutt Williams					Shia LaBeouf
Harold Oxley					John Hurt

Literature

Adult novels

The first novelization was of *Raiders of the Lost Ark*, written by Campbell Black and published by Ballantine Books in April 1981. It was followed by *Indiana Jones and the Temple of Doom*, written by James Kahn and published by Ballantine in May 1984. Finally, they published *Indiana Jones and the Last Crusade* in May 1989. It was the first Indy book by Rob MacGregor. MacGregor was awarded the job after helping an editor on another project. Neither the editor nor LucasFilm were aware of MacGregor's interest in history and archaeology. A fan of the first two films, MacGregor admitted writing the novelization made him "somewhat disappointed with [the third]. That's because I took the script and expanded it to novel length [and] adding scenes while Spielberg took the same script and trimmed a few scenes to tighten the story. So, for me, it was all very familiar when I saw the movie, but it seemed somehow to be missing something."

German Fantasy and SF author Wolfgang Hohlbein wrote eight novels from 1990—1993 published by the Goldmann Verlag, but none of these were translated into English. Hohlbein set his books from 1938—1944, except for the first which he set in 1929 and 1932. Lucas had no involvement in this series.

Meanwhile, Lucas asked Rob MacGregor to continue writing original novels for Bantam Books. They chose to make them prequels set in the 1920s (after Indy graduates from college), so to not interfere with the films. Lucas only permitted Marcus Brody to appear. Lucas also told MacGregor to base the books on real myths, but except for the deletion of a sex scene, MacGregor was given total creative freedom. Barring Stonehenge, MacGregor chose locations he had visited in the past. His six books -- *Indiana Jones and the Peril at Delphi*, *Indiana Jones and the Dance of the Giants*, *Indiana Jones and the Seven Veils*, *Indiana Jones and the Genesis Deluge*, *Indiana Jones and the Unicorn's Legacy*, and *Indiana Jones and the Interior World* -- were published from February 1991—November 1992. The fourth book, *The Genesis Deluge* (Feb 1992), featuring Noah's Ark, was the best-selling novel. MacGregor felt it "had a strong following among religious-oriented people [...] because they tend to take the Noah's Ark story to heart and think of it as history and archaeological fact, rather than myth. They also see Indy as one of their own, even though he's actually quite an iconoclast [...] However, Indy follows the trail and indeed finds 'an ark' on Mount Ararat." MacGregor's own favorite of his books was the preceding third book *The Seven Veils*. This featured real-life explorer Percy Fawcett, and the tragic death of Indy's wife, Deirdre Campbell. Deirdre, a red haired student of Indy at the University of London, dies in the book's climactic plane crash.

Martin Caidin wrote the next two novels in Bantam's series, *Indiana Jones and the Sky Pirates* and *Indiana Jones and the White Witch*. These both feature Gale Parker (like Deirdre Campbell, a red haired woman) as Indiana's sidekick, and also introduced afterwords to the series, regarding the novel's historical context. Caidin became ill, so Max McCoy took over in 1995 and wrote the final four novels,

Indiana Jones and the Philosopher's Stone, *Indiana Jones and the Dinosaur Eggs*, *Indiana Jones and the Hollow Earth*, and *Indiana Jones and the Secret of the Sphinx*. McCoy set his books nearer to *Raiders*, which informed his characterization of Indy. "The *Raiders* Indy was a bit darker [...] Not evil, just a shade rougher, and a little closer to Belloq than he would like to admit. In *Raiders*, Indy had to decide to be a hero," he said. McCoy gave a sample to his editors, featuring the crystal skull, which became the prologue of the first book. The skull became a recurring story, which concludes when Indy gives it up in the final novel. McCoy spent a longer time researching his novels, and Lucas's involvement was limited. LucasFilm also had to censor sexual or outlandish elements of his novels, in order to make McCoy's adult sensibilities appeal to younger readers, and they also rejected time travel in the final book because it was too science-fictional. Sallah, Lao Che, Rene Belloq and the Nazis made appearances, and McCoy also pitted Indy against Benito Mussolini's fascists and the Japanese. Indy has a doomed romance with Alecia Dunstin, a red-haired librarian at the British Museum, in this cycle. A novel involving the spear of destiny was dropped because Dark Horse Comics was developing the idea.

IGN journalist Scott Chitwood felt, "Bantam never marketed [the books] very well and many people never knew they existed." He asked former Bantam editor Tom Dupree in 2000, why they were not published in hardback. He answered, "Indy is just a better educated, more erudite, more human Doc Savage. Who wants to pay $22 for an adventure novel? Keep them at the paperback price, then if Indy 4 gets closer to reality, maybe we might rethink." In February 2008, the novelizations of the first three films were published in one edition. James Rollins' *Kingdom of the Crystal Skull* novelization arrived the following May. Children's novelizations of all four films were published by Scholastic in 2008. MacGregor is writing new books for Ballantine for early 2009, as is Steve Perry, whose *Army of the Dead* is due April 28, 2009. In May 2009, a new "middle grade" series entitled *Untold Adventures* will begin. The first two books are entitled *Pyramid of the Sorcerer* and *Mystery of Mount Sinai*.

Indiana Jones (Prequels) - Bantam Books

This series of 12 books was published by Bantam Books between 1991 and 1999. The books were geared toward an adult / young adult audience and are prequels to the storyline of the film series, as they are set in the 1920s and early 1930s.

- *Indiana Jones and the Peril at Delphi* (Feb 1991) - by Rob Macgregor
- *Indiana Jones and the Dance of the Giants* (June 1991) - by Rob Macgregor
- *Indiana Jones and the Seven Veils* (Dec 1991) - by Rob Macgregor
- *Indiana Jones and the Genesis Deluge* (Feb 1992) - by Rob Macgregor
- *Indiana Jones and the Unicorn's Legacy* (Sept 1992) - by Rob Macgregor
- *Indiana Jones and the Interior World* (1992) - by Rob Macgregor
- *Indiana Jones and the Sky Pirates* (Dec 1993) - by Martin Caidin
- *Indiana Jones and the White Witch* (1994) - by Martin Caidin
- *Indiana Jones and the Philosopher's Stone* (1995) - by Max McCoy

- *Indiana Jones and the Dinosaur Eggs* (1996) - by Max McCoy
- *Indiana Jones and the Hollow Earth* (1997) - by Max McCoy
- *Indiana Jones and the Secret of the Sphinx* (1999) - by Max McCoy

Indiana Jones - Del Rey

- *Indiana Jones and the Army of the Dead* (2009) - by Steve Perry

Find Your Fate

There were eleven Indiana Jones books released in the *Find Your Fate* line, written by various authors. These books were similar to the *Choose Your Own Adventure* series, allowing the reader to select from options that change the outcome of the story. Nearly the entire 17 book Ballantine Books Find Your Fate series was dedicated to stories within the world of Indiana Jones, with the exception of books #10 - #15 which centered around either Morgan Swift (# 10 & 15) or James Bond (# 11-14).

- *Indiana Jones and the Curse of Horror Island* (June 1984) - R. L. Stine
- *Indiana Jones and the Lost Treasure of Sheba* (June 1984) - Rose Estes
- *Indiana Jones and the Giants of the Silver Tower* (Aug 1984) - R. L. Stine
- *Indiana Jones and the Eye of the Fates* (Aug 1984) - Richard Wenk
- *Indiana Jones and the Cup of the Vampire* (Oct 1984) - Andy Helfer
- *Indiana Jones and the Legion of Death* (Dec 1984) - Richard Wenk
- *Indiana Jones and the Cult of the Mummy's Crypt* (Feb 1985) - R. L. Stine
- *Indiana Jones and the Dragon of Vengeance* (Apr 1985) - Megan Stine and H. William Stine
- *Indiana Jones and the Gold of Genghis Khan* (May 1985) - Ellen Weiss
- *Indiana Jones and the Ape Slaves of Howling Island* (1986) - R. L. Stine
- *Indiana Jones and the Mask of the Elephant* (Feb 1987) - Megan Stine and H. William Stine

Young Indiana Jones

Random House

- *Young Indiana Jones and the Plantation Treasure* - by William McCay
- *Young Indiana Jones and the Tomb of Terror* - by Les Martin
- *Young Indiana Jones and the Circle of Death* - by William McCay
- *Young Indiana Jones and the Secret City* - by Les Martin
- *Young Indiana Jones and the Princess of Peril* - by Les Martin
- *Young Indiana Jones and the Gypsy Revenge* - by Les Martin
- *Young Indiana Jones and the Ghostly Riders* - by William McCay
- *Young Indiana Jones and the Curse of Ruby Cross* - by William McCay
- *Young Indiana Jones and the Titanic Adventure* - by Les Martin
- *Young Indiana Jones and the Lost Gold of Durango* - by Megan Stine and H. William Stine

- *Young Indiana Jones and the Face of the Dragon* - by William McCay
- *Young Indiana Jones and the Journey to the Underworld* - by Megan Stine and H. William Stine
- *Young Indiana Jones and the Mountain of Fire* - by William McCay
- *Young Indiana Jones and the Pirates' Loot* - by J.N. Fox
- *Young Indiana Jones and the Eye of the Tiger* - by William McCay
- *Young Indiana Jones and the Mask of the Madman* - by Megan Stine and H. William Stine
- *Young Indiana Jones and the Ring of Power* - Megan Stine
- *The Young Indiana Jones Chronicles: The Mummy's Curse* - by Megan Stine and H. William Stine
- *The Young Indiana Jones Chronicles: Field of Death* - by Les Martin
- *The Young Indiana Jones Chronicles: Safari Sleuth* - by A.L. Singer
- *The Young Indiana Jones Chronicles: The Secret Peace* - by William McCay
- *The Young Indiana Jones Chronicles: The Trek of Doom* - by Les Martin
- *The Young Indiana Jones Chronicles: Revolution!* - by Gavin Scott
- *The Young Indiana Jones Chronicles: Race to Danger* - by Stephanie Calmenson
- *The Young Indiana Jones Chronicles: Prisoner of War* - by Sam Mclean

Bantam Books

The Young Indiana Jones Chronicles:

- *The Valley of The Kings* - by Richard Brightfield
- *South of the Border* - by Richard Brightfield
- *Revolution in Russia* - by Richard Brightfield
- *Masters of the Louvre* - by Richard Brightfield
- *African Safari* - by Richard Brightfield
- *Behind the Great Wall* - by Richard Brightfield
- *The Roaring Twenties* - by Richard Brightfield
- *The Irish Rebellion* - by Richard Brightfield

Ballantine Books

Young Indiana Jones:

- *The Mata Hari Affair* - by James Luceno
- *The Mummy's Curse* - by Parker Smith

Graphic novels

- *The Curse of the Jackal* - by Dan Barry
- *The Search for the Oryx* - by Dan Barry
- *The Peril of the Fort* - by Dan Barry

Non-fiction books

- *Lost Diaries of Young Indiana Jones* by Eric D. Weiner
- *The Young Indiana Jones Chronicles: On the Set and Behind the Scenes* by Dan Madsen

- *Indiana Jones Explores Ancient Egypt* - by John Malam
- *Indiana Jones Explores Ancient Rome* - by John Malam
- *Indiana Jones Explores Ancient Greece* - by John Malam
- *Indiana Jones Explores The Vikings* - by John Malam
- *Indiana Jones Explores The Incas* - by John Malam
- *Indiana Jones Explores The Aztecs* - by John Malam

Comic books

Main article: Indiana Jones comic books

Video games

The first Indiana Jones video game was a 1982 adaptation of *Raiders of the Lost Ark*, released on the Atari 2600. Atari released *Indiana Jones and the Temple of Doom* in 1985. In 1988, an NES version of *Temple of Doom* was released. LucasArts released two versions of *Indiana Jones and the Last Crusade*, entitled *The Action Game* and *The Graphic Adventure*. An NES version of *The Last Crusade* was released in 1991. The final adaptation of the films, until 2008, was *Indiana Jones' Greatest Adventures*, released on the Super Nintendo Entertainment System in 1994. In 2008, LucasArts released Lego Indiana Jones: The Original Adventures, which was based on the original three movies.

LucasArts released the first original Indiana Jones game, *Indiana Jones and the Fate of Atlantis*, in 1992, which was a personal computer game. A sequel, entitled *Indiana Jones and the Iron Phoenix*, was intended for a 1995 release, but was cancelled. *Indiana Jones and His Desktop Adventures* followed instead in 1996. LucasArts released *Indiana Jones and the Infernal Machine* in 1999 on the PC, and it was also released on the Nintendo 64 and the Game Boy Color by 2001. The game featured the return of Sophia Hapgood, Indy's sidekick from *Fate of Atlantis*. *Indiana Jones and the Emperor's Tomb*, a prequel to *Temple of Doom*, was released on the PlayStation 2, Xbox, Apple Macintosh and Microsoft Windows in 2003. Another game with the title *Indiana Jones and the Staff of Kings* was released in June 2009 for the Nintendo DS, Wii, PSP and PS2.

Attractions

George Lucas has collaborated with Walt Disney Imagineering on four occasions to create Indiana Jones attractions for Disney theme parks worldwide:

Action on the set of the "Indiana Jones Epic Stunt Spectacular!"

- The "Indiana Jones Epic Stunt Spectacular!" show opened at the Disney's Hollywood Studios in Lake Buena Vista, Florida, in 1989.
- The "Indiana Jones et le Temple du Péril" rollercoaster opened at Disneyland Paris in Marne-la-Vallee, France, in 1993.
- The "Indiana Jones and the Temple of the Forbidden Eye" opened at Disneyland in Anaheim, California, in 1995.
- The "Indiana Jones and the Temple of the Crystal Skull" opened at Tokyo DisneySea in Chiba, Japan, with the park, in 2001.

Merchandise

Toy lines

Further information: LEGO Indiana Jones

For the holiday season following the June 1981 debut of *Raiders of the Lost Ark*, Kenner produced a 12-inch-tall "Authentically styled Action Figure" of Indiana Jones. The next spring they delivered nine smaller-scale (3-3/4") action figures, three playsets, and replicas of the German "Desert Convoy Truck [1]," and Indy's Arabian horse, all based on characters and situations from the *Raiders* movie. They also offered a Kenner-branded *Raiders* board game. In conjunction with the theatrical release of *Temple of Doom* (1984), TSR, Inc. put out miniature metal versions of twelve characters from both *ToD* and *Raiders* for a role playing game. LJN Toys Ltd. released just three six-inch action figures for *Temple of Doom* in 1984: Indy, Mola Ram, and the Giant Thugee; there were plans for the addition of Willie Scott and Short Round, and also a mine car racing set, but these followups were never made available. The third Indy feature film, *The Last Crusade* (1989), saw *no* toy merchandise tie-ins, but by 1993 Horizon filled the void with highly detailed vinyl model kits of Indy and his father, Henry, Sr., while in 1995 Micro Machines released a box set of ten die-cast toy vehicles from all the films to that point. Micro Machines also considered a mini. playset that was never made available to the buying public. Toys McCoy released a Japanese-market-only limited edition (3000 units) 12-inch Indy and his horse from *Raiders* in 1999. In January 2001, Walt Disney Parks and Resorts sold new and exclusive action figures and vehicle models, and a second wave followed in August 2003. This included G.I. Joe versions of Indy, including an African-American styled toy, to honor the black performers at their stunt shows.

Hasbro released toys based on *Raiders of the Lost Ark* and *Kingdom of the Crystal Skull* on May 1, 2008. Figure waves including characters from *The Last Crusade,* and *Temple of Doom* followed later in the year, but ended up being distributed on a very limited basis, and proved rather difficult for collectors to find. The new toy line consists of 3 3/4-inch sized, highly articulated figures (each packed with a "Hidden Relic" artifact), supporting vehicles, and an Akator playset. A run of eight large (12-inch-tall) action figures was also issued, along with a series of "Adventure Heroes" aimed at young children. Die-cast vehicles, and some role-playing items rounded out the line. Hasbro ran several incentive mail-away offers requiring proof of purchase to receive an exclusive one sixth-scale (sized for 12-inch figures) Ark of the Covenant, an "Adventure Heroes" Indy with his horse from the first film, or a crystal skeleton action figure from the fourth film. Hasbro announced the cancellation of the line in the fall of 2008, due to poor overall sales, coupled with a down economy in the U.S. . Sideshow Collectibles, Gentle Giant, Diamond Select Toys and Kotobukiya also earned the Indiana Jones licensing rights in 2008. Lego will release eight play sets to coincide with the fourth film. Only half of them are based on *Kingdom of the Crystal Skull*: three are based on *Raiders* and another is based on *Crusade*.

Merchandise featuring franchise cross-overs include a spoofy Mr. Potato Head *Taters Of The Lost Ark* set by Hasbro, Mickey Mouse as Indiana Jones (available only in Disney parks), and a Muppets-brand Adventure Kermit action figure, produced by Palisades Toys, based on the frog's appearance in the Disney World stunt show as seen in *The Muppets at Walt Disney World* (although for legal reasons, the producers and figure's packaging made it clear that "Adventure Kermit" was in no way affiliated with Indiana Jones; the item nonetheless appears in DK's *Indiana Jones: The Ultimate Guide*, published in 2008).

Role playing games

Main article: Indiana Jones (role-playing game)

Pinball

Main article: Indiana Jones: The Pinball Adventure

A pinball machine based on the first three films was released in 1993. Stern Pinball released a new edition in 2008, which featured all four movies.

References

- Rinzler, J.W.; Laurent Bouzereau (2008). *The Complete Making of Indiana Jones*. Random House. ISBN 9780091926618.
- Hearn, Marcus (2005). *The Cinema of George Lucas*. New York: Harry N. Abrams Inc, Publishers. ISBN 0-8109-4968-7.
- McBride, Joseph (1997). *Steven Spielberg*. New York City: Faber and Faber. ISBN 0-571-19177-0.

External links

- Official site [1]
  - Indiana Jones Shop [1]
- TheRaider.net [2]
- Indiana Jones series [3] at Box Office Mojo
- Indiana Jones, an external wiki [4]

Han Solo

Han Solo

Han Solo	
Position	Captain of the *Millennium Falcon*, general in the Rebel Alliance/New Republic, smuggler
Homeworld	Corellia
Species	Human
Gender	Male
Affiliation	Rebel Alliance, New Republic, Galactic Alliance
Portrayed by	Harrison Ford (films) Neil Ross (*Star Wars: Rogue Squadron*, *Star Wars: Force Commander*, *Star Wars: Masters of Teräs Käsi*) Lex Lang (*Star Wars: Rogue Squadron III - Rebel Strike*, *Star Wars: Battlefront 2*) John Armstrong (*Star Wars: Empire at War*, *Star Wars Battlefront: Renegade Squadron'*) *Perry King (radio dramas)*

Han Solo, played by Harrison Ford, is a fictional smuggler and "reckless mercenary" in the *Star Wars* franchise. Introduced in the film *Star Wars Episode IV: A New Hope* (1977), Solo and his Wookiee first mate, Chewbacca (Peter Mayhew), become involved in the Rebel Alliance against the authoritarian Galactic Empire. Over the course of the *Star Wars* franchise, Solo becomes a chief figure in the Alliance and succeeding galactic governments. *Star Wars* creator George Lucas described Solo as "a loner who realizes the importance of being part of a group and helping for the common good."

Han remains one of cinema's most revered movie characters. The American Film Institute ranked Solo as the 14th greatest film hero. He was also deemed the 4th greatest movie character of all-time by *Empire* magazine. Entertainment Weekly ranked the character 7th on their list of *The All-Time Coolest Heroes in Pop Culture*. On their list of the *100 Greatest Fictional Characters*, Fandomania.com ranked Solo at number 15.

Depiction

At the beginning of *A New Hope*, Solo and Chewbacca are desperate to pay off a debt to Jabba the Hutt. Solo accepts a charter to transport Obi-Wan Kenobi (Alec Guinness), Luke Skywalker (Mark Hamill), C-3PO (Anthony Daniels), and R2-D2 (Kenny Baker) to Alderaan in Han's ship, the *Millennium Falcon*; when they arrive, they find Alderaan has been destroyed by the Death Star, and the *Falcon* is captured. Enticed by the likelihood of a substantial reward, Solo and Chewbacca help Skywalker rescue Princess Leia (Carrie Fisher), held captive aboard the station. After escaping and delivering Skywalker, Leia, and the droids to the Rebels, Solo and Chewbacca receive payment for their services and depart; Solo believes the Rebels' plan to attack the Death Star is "suicide." However, Solo soon has a change of heart and returns to aid in the attack, ultimately enabling Skywalker to fire the shot that destroys the Death Star. Following this, Han accepts a position as Captain with the Rebel Alliance.

When the Empire attacks the Rebels' base on Hoth in *The Empire Strikes Back* (1980), Solo transports Chewbacca, Leia, and C-3PO to Cloud City for safety and repairs to the *Falcon*. The bounty hunter Boba Fett (Jeremy Bulloch) tracks the *Falcon* to Cloud City, and Darth Vader (David Prowse/James Earl Jones) forces Cloud City's administrator, Lando Calrissian (Billy Dee Williams), to help capture Solo. Leia confesses her love of Solo shortly before he is frozen in carbonite for delivery to Jabba the Hutt. Although Calrissian helps free Vader's other captives, they do not succeed in releasing Solo. However, Leia infiltrates Jabba's palace at the beginning of *Return of the Jedi* (1983) and frees Solo. Reunited with the Rebels, Solo rejoins the Alliance and is commissioned as a general. Along with Leia and Chewbacca, he leads a team in deactivating the shields protecting the Empire's second Death Star. Aided by the indigenous Ewoks, Solo and the Rebels succeed in overcoming the Imperial garrison, allowing the Rebels' space forces to destroy the Empire's battlestation.

Brian Daley wrote a series of novels, the first published in 1979, exploring Solo and Chewbecca's smuggling adventures, and Ann C. Crispin's *Han Solo Trilogy* (1997-1998) further develops the character's backstory. Crispin's books depict Solo as a beggar and pickpocket for much of his youth. He becomes a pilot and, in the process of undermining a religious fraud, frees and falls in love with Bria Tharen. Tharen, however, disappears soon before Solo joins the Imperial Navy. Solo loses his commission and is cashiered when he refuses an order to skin Chewbacca, who had commandeered a ship carrying Wookiee children destined for slavery; Chewbacca, in turn, swears a life-debt to Solo. The two become a prominent smuggling team, and help repel an Imperial blockade of a Hutt moon. Solo soon thereafter wins the *Millennium Falcon* from Lando Calrissian in a card tournament. Tharen, who has become a Rebel agent, reappears and asks for Solo, Chewbacca, and Calrissian's help in attacking a slave colony. After succeeding, Tharen's troopers steal the smuggler's valuables to aid the Rebel Alliance. Desperate to recoup their losses, Solo and Chewbacca accept a smuggling job from Jabba the Hutt. However, Imperials intercept the *Falcon*, forcing the smugglers to jettison their cargo. This loss is the debt Solo and Chewbacca owe the Hutt crime lord at the beginning of *A New Hope*.

Solo plays a central role in the years following Emperor Palpatine's death in *Return of the Jedi*. In *The Courtship of Princess Leia* (1995), he resigns his commission to pursue Leia, whom he eventually marries. Han and Leia have three children together: twins Jaina and Jacen and their younger brother, Anakin. Chewbacca dies saving Anakin's life in *Vector Prime* (1999). Solo takes his companion's death hard, sinking into alcoholism and depression. He takes his anger and grief out on his family, alienating them and returning to his loner lifestyle. In *Star by Star* (2001), Anakin dies as well, compounding Han's despair. By the end of the series, however, he accepts Anakin's and Chewbacca's deaths and repairs his relationship with his family. In the *Legacy of the Force* series, Jacen falls to the dark side of the Force, eventually becoming the Sith lord Darth Caedus. Although Solo disowns Jacen, he and Leia adopt Jacen's daughter, Allana, after Jacen's death.

Influence and critical reaction

Solo is a reckless smuggler with a sarcastic wit; he is "a very practical guy" and considers himself "a materialist." However, the adventures in the first *Star Wars* movie evoke his compassion, a trait "he didn't know he possessed."

Prince of Persia producer Ben Mattes explained that their "inspiration was anything Harrison Ford has ever done: Indiana Jones, Han Solo." The Japanese manga and anime anti-hero Space Adventure Cobra has been compared by reviewers to Solo. In preparing to play James T. Kirk for the 2009 *Star Trek* film, Chris Pine drew inspiration from Ford's depictions of Solo and Indiana Jones, highlighting their humor and "accidental hero" traits.

Merchandising

Solo has been merchandised in multiple media, including action figures, video games, and other collectibles. A Han Solo action figure with "human proportions" was released in 1977 for *A New Hope*, while a figure created for the films' mid-1990s re-release is "unrealistically muscled."

See also

- Han shot first

External links

- Han Solo [1] in the *Star Wars* Databank
- Han Solo [2] on Wookieepedia: a *Star Wars* Wiki [4]
- Han Solo [3] at the Internet Movie Database
- Han Solo [4] at The World of Star Wars

Star Wars

Star Wars is an American epic space opera franchise conceived by George Lucas. The first film in the franchise was originally released on May 25, 1977, by 20th Century Fox, and became a worldwide pop culture phenomenon, followed by two sequels, released at three-year intervals. Sixteen years after the release of the trilogy's final film, the first in a new prequel trilogy of films was released, again released at three-year intervals, with the final film released on May 19, 2005.

The *Star Wars* logo, as seen in all films.

As of 2008, the overall box office revenue generated by the six *Star Wars* films has totalled approximately $5.51 billion, making it the third-highest-grossing film series, behind only the *James Bond* and *Harry Potter* films.

The *Star Wars* film series has spawned other media including books, television series, video games, and comic books. These supplements to the film trilogies comprise the *Star Wars* Expanded Universe, and have resulted in significant development of the series' fictional universe. These media kept the franchise going in the interim between the film trilogies. In 2008, *Star Wars: The Clone Wars* was released to theaters as the first ever worldwide theatrical *Star Wars* film outside of the main trilogies. It was the franchise's first animated film, and was intended as an introduction to the Expanded Universe series of the same name, a 3D CGI animated series based on a previous 2D animated series of a similar name.

Setting

The events depicted in *Star Wars* media take place in a fictional galaxy. Many species of alien creatures (often humanoid) are depicted. Robotic droids are also commonplace and are generally built to serve their owners. Space travel is common, and many planets in the galaxy are members of a Galactic Republic, later reorganized as the Galactic Empire.

One of the prominent elements of *Star Wars* is the "Force", which is an omnipresent form of energy which can be harnessed by those with that ability. It is described in the first produced film as "an energy field created by all living things [that] surrounds us, penetrates us, [and] binds the galaxy together." The Force allows users to perform a variety of supernatural feats (such as telekinesis, clairvoyance, precognition, and mind control) and also can amplify certain physical traits, such as speed and reflexes; these abilities can vary from user to user and can be improved through training. While the Force can be used for good, it has a dark side that, when pursued, imbues users with hatred, aggression, and malevolence. The six films feature the Jedi, who use the Force for good, and the Sith, who use the dark side for evil in an attempt to take over the galaxy. In the Expanded Universe, many dark side users are Dark Jedi rather than Sith, mainly because of the "Rule of Two" (see Sith Origin).

Feature films

The film series began with *Star Wars*, released on May 25, 1977. This was followed by two sequels: *The Empire Strikes Back*, released on May 21, 1980, and *Return of the Jedi*, released on May 25, 1983. The opening crawl of the sequels disclosed that they were numbered as "Episode V" and "Episode VI" respectively, though the films were generally advertised solely under their subtitles. Though the first film in the series was simply titled *Star Wars*, it later had the subtitle *Episode IV: A New Hope* added to distinguish it from its sequels and prequels.

In 1997, to correspond with the 20th anniversary of the release of *Star Wars*, Lucas released "Special Editions" of the three films to theaters. The re-releases featured alterations to the original films, primarily motivated by the improvement of CGI and other special effects technologies, which allowed visuals that were not possible to achieve at the time of the original filmmaking. Lucas continued to make changes to the original trilogy for subsequent releases, such as the first ever DVD release of the trilogy on September 21, 2004.

More than two decades after the release of the original *Star Wars*, the series continued with the long-awaited prequel trilogy; consisting of *Episode I: The Phantom Menace*, released on May 19, 1999, *Episode II: Attack of the Clones*, released on May 16, 2002, and *Episode III: Revenge of the Sith*, released on May 19, 2005.

Plot overview

The prequel trilogy follows the early life of Anakin Skywalker, who is discovered by the Jedi Knight Qui-Gon Jinn. He is believed to be the "Chosen One" foretold by Jedi prophecy to bring balance to the Force. The Jedi Council, led by Yoda, sense that his future is clouded with fear, but reluctantly allow Qui-Gon's apprentice Obi-Wan Kenobi to train Anakin after Qui-Gon is killed by the Sith Lord Darth Maul. At the same time, the planet Naboo is under attack, and its ruler, Queen Padmé Amidala, seeks the assistance of the Jedi to repel the attack. The Sith Lord Darth Sidious secretly planned the attack to give his alter-ego, Senator Palpatine, a pretense to overthrow the Supreme Chancellor of the Galactic Republic. The remainder of the prequel trilogy chronicles Anakin's gradual fall to the dark side of the Force as he fights in the Clone Wars, which Palpatine secretly engineers in order to destroy the Republic and lure Anakin into his service. Anakin and Padmé fall in love and secretly wed, and eventually Padmé becomes pregnant. Anakin has a prophetic vision of Padmé dying in childbirth, and Palpatine convinces him that the dark side holds the power to save her life; desperate, Anakin submits to the dark side and takes the Sith name Darth Vader. While Palpatine re-organizes the Republic into the tyrannical Galactic Empire — appointing himself Emperor for life — Vader participates in the extermination of the Jedi Order, culminating in a lightsaber battle between himself and Obi-Wan. After defeating his former apprentice, Obi-Wan leaves Vader for dead. However, Palpatine arrives shortly after to save him and put him into a mechanical suit of black armor that keeps him alive. At the same time, Padmé dies while giving birth to twins Luke and Leia. The twins are hidden from Vader and are not told who their true parents are.

The original trilogy begins 19 years later as Vader nears completion of the massive Death Star space station, which will allow the Empire to crush the Rebel Alliance, which has formed to combat Palpatine's tyranny. Vader captures Princess Leia Organa, who has stolen the plans to the Death Star and hidden them in the astromech droid R2-D2. R2-D2, along with his counterpart C-3PO, escape to the planet Tatooine. There, the droids are purchased by Luke Skywalker, the son of Anakin, and his step-uncle and aunt. While Luke is cleaning R2-D2, he accidentally triggers a message put into the droid by Leia, who asks for assistance from Obi-Wan. Luke later assists the droids in finding the Jedi Knight, who is now passing as an old hermit under the alias Ben Kenobi. When Luke asks about his father, Obi-Wan tells him that Anakin was a great Jedi who was betrayed and murdered by Vader. Obi-Wan and Luke hire the smuggler Han Solo and his Wookiee co-pilot Chewbacca to take them to Alderaan, Leia's homeworld, which they eventually find has been destroyed by the Death Star. Once onboard the space station, Obi-Wan allows himself to be killed in a showdown with Vader; his sacrifice allows the group to escape with the plans that help the rebels destroy the Death Star.

Three years later, Luke travels to find Yoda and start his Jedi training, but is interrupted when Vader lures him into a trap by capturing Han and the others. Vader reveals that he is Luke's father and attempts to turn him to the dark side. Luke escapes, and returns to his training with Yoda, who by this time is on his deathbed. Before he passes away, Yoda informs Luke that he must face his father before he can become a Jedi, and that Leia is his twin sister. As the rebels attack the second Death Star, Luke confronts Vader as Palpatine watches; both Sith Lords intend to turn Luke to the dark side and take him as their apprentice. During the subsequent lightsaber duel, Luke succumbs to his anger and brutally overpowers Vader, but controls himself at the last minute; realizing that he is about to suffer his father's fate, he spares Vader's life and proudly declares his allegiance to the Jedi. An enraged Palpatine then attempts to kill Luke, a sight that moves Vader to turn on and kill his master, suffering mortal wounds in the process. Redeemed, Anakin Skywalker dies in his son's arms. Luke becomes a full-fledged Jedi, and the Rebels destroy the second Death Star and, with it, the Empire.

Cast and characters

Further information: List of Star Wars films cast members and List of Star Wars characters

Character	Film					
	The Phantom Menace	***Attack of the Clones***	***Revenge of the Sith***	***A New Hope***	***The Empire Strikes Back***	***Return of the Jedi***
Anakin Skywalker / Darth Vader	Jake Lloyd	Hayden Christensen	Hayden Christensen James Earl Jones (voice only; Darth Vader)	David Prowse James Earl Jones (voice only)		**Vader**: David Prowse James Earl Jones (voice only) **Anakin**: Sebastian Shaw Hayden Christensen (2004 DVD release)
Obi-Wan Kenobi	Ewan McGregor			Alec Guinness		
R2-D2	Kenny Baker					
C-3PO	Anthony Daniels					
Yoda	Frank Oz (voice only)				Frank Oz (voice only)	
Palpatine	Ian McDiarmid				Clive Revill (voice only) Ian McDiarmid (2004 DVD release)	Ian McDiarmid
Qui-Gon Jinn	Liam Neeson	Liam Neeson (voice only)				
Nute Gunray	Silas Carson					
Padmé Amidala	Natalie Portman					
Captain Panaka	Hugh Quarshie					

<table>
<tr><td>Sio Bibble</td><td colspan="3">Oliver Ford Davies</td><td colspan="3"></td></tr>
<tr><td>Sabé</td><td>Keira Knightley</td><td colspan="5"></td></tr>
<tr><td>Jar Jar Binks</td><td colspan="3">Ahmed Best (voice only)</td><td colspan="3"></td></tr>
<tr><td>Boss Nass</td><td>Brian Blessed (voice only)</td><td></td><td>Brian Blessed (voice only)</td><td colspan="3"></td></tr>
<tr><td>Darth Maul</td><td>Ray Park
Peter Serafinowicz (voice only)</td><td colspan="5"></td></tr>
<tr><td>Watto</td><td colspan="2">Andy Secombe (voice only)</td><td colspan="4"></td></tr>
<tr><td>Sebulba</td><td>Lewis MacLeod (voice only)</td><td colspan="5"></td></tr>
<tr><td>Shmi Skywalker</td><td colspan="2">Pernilla August</td><td colspan="4"></td></tr>
<tr><td>Jabba the Hutt</td><td>Larry Ward (voice only)</td><td colspan="2"></td><td>Larry Ward (voice only)</td><td></td><td>Larry Ward (voice only)</td></tr>
<tr><td>Bib Fortuna</td><td>Alan Ruscoe
Matthew Wood (voice only)</td><td colspan="4"></td><td>Erik Bauersfeld
Michael Carter (voice only)</td></tr>
<tr><td>Chancellor Valorum</td><td>Terence Stamp</td><td colspan="5"></td></tr>
<tr><td>Mace Windu</td><td colspan="3">Samuel L. Jackson</td><td colspan="3"></td></tr>
<tr><td>Ki-Adi-Mundi</td><td colspan="3">Silas Carson</td><td colspan="3"></td></tr>
<tr><td>Captain Typho</td><td></td><td colspan="2">Jay Laga'aia</td><td colspan="3"></td></tr>
<tr><td>Bail Organa</td><td></td><td colspan="2">Jimmy Smits</td><td colspan="3"></td></tr>
<tr><td>Zam Wesell</td><td></td><td>Leeanna Walsman</td><td colspan="4"></td></tr>
<tr><td>Jango Fett</td><td></td><td>Temuera Morrison</td><td colspan="4"></td></tr>
<tr><td>Dexter Jettster</td><td></td><td>Ronald Falk (voice only)</td><td colspan="4"></td></tr>
<tr><td>Boba Fett</td><td></td><td>Daniel Logan</td><td></td><td colspan="3">Jeremy Bulloch
Jason Wingreen (voice only)
Temuera Morrison (voice only; 2004 DVD release)</td></tr>
<tr><td>Owen Lars</td><td></td><td colspan="2">Joel Edgerton</td><td>Phil Brown</td><td colspan="2"></td></tr>
<tr><td>Beru</td><td></td><td colspan="2">Bonnie Piesse</td><td>Shelagh Fraser</td><td colspan="2"></td></tr>
</table>

Cliegg Lars		Jack Thompson				
Count Dooku		Christopher Lee				
General Grievous			Matthew Wood (voice only)			
Chewbacca			Peter Mayhew			
Luke Skywalker			Aidan Barton	Mark Hamill		
Leia Organa			Aidan Barton	Carrie Fisher		
Grand Moff Tarkin			Wayne Pygram	Peter Cushing		
Han Solo				Harrison Ford		
Wedge Antilles				Denis Lawson		
Admiral Piett					Kenneth Colley	
Lando Calrissian					Billy Dee Williams	
Admiral Ackbar						Timothy M. Rose Erik Bauersfeld (voice only)
Wicket						Warwick Davis

Themes

See also: Philosophy and religion in Star Wars and Force (Star Wars)

Star Wars features elements such as knights, witches, and princesses that are related to archetypes of the fantasy genre. The *Star Wars* world, unlike science-fiction and fantasy films that featured sleek and futuristic settings, was portrayed as dirty and grimy. Lucas' vision of a "used future" was further popularized in the science fiction-horror films *Alien*, which was set on a dirty space freighter; *Mad Max 2*, which is set in a post-apocalyptic desert; and *Blade Runner*, which is set in a crumbling, dirty city of the future. Lucas made a conscious effort to parallel scenes and dialogue between films, and especially to parallel the journeys of Luke Skywalker with that of his father Anakin when making the prequels.

Technical information

All six films of the *Star Wars* series were shot in an aspect ratio of 2.35:1. The original trilogy was shot with anamorphic lenses. Episodes IV and V were shot in Panavision, while Episode VI was shot in Joe Dunton Camera (JDC) scope. Episode I was shot with Hawk anamorphic lenses on Arriflex cameras, and Episodes II and III were shot with Sony's CineAlta high-definition digital cameras. Lucas hired Ben Burtt to oversee the sound effects on *A New Hope*.

Burtt's accomplishment was such that the Academy of Motion Picture Arts and Sciences presented him with a Special Achievement Award because it had no award at the time for the work he had done. Lucasfilm developed the THX sound reproduction standard for *Return of the Jedi.* John Williams composed the scores for all six films. Lucas' design for *Star Wars* involved a grand musical sound, with leitmotifs for different characters and important concepts. Williams' *Star Wars* title theme has become one of the most famous and well-known musical compositions in modern music history.

The technical lightsaber choreography for the original trilogy was developed by Hollywood sword-master Bob Anderson. Anderson trained actor Mark Hamill (Luke Skywalker) and performed all the sword stunts as Darth Vader during the lightsaber duels in *The Empire Strikes Back* and *Return of the Jedi*, wearing Vader's costume. Anderson's role in the original *Star Wars* trilogy was highlighted in the film *Reclaiming the Blade*, where he shares his experiences as the fight choreographer developing the lightsaber techniques for the movies.

Production history

Original trilogy

George Lucas, the creator of *Star Wars*.

In 1971, Universal Studios agreed to make *American Graffiti* and *Star Wars* in a two-picture contract, although *Star Wars* was later rejected in its early concept stages. *American Graffiti* was completed in 1973 and, a few months later, Lucas wrote a short summary called "The Journal of the Whills", which told the tale of the training of apprentice C.J. Thorpe as a "Jedi-Bendu" space commando by the legendary Mace Windy. Frustrated that his story was too difficult to understand, Lucas then wrote a 13-page treatment called *The Star Wars*, which was a loose remake of Akira Kurosawa's *The Hidden Fortress*. By 1974, he had expanded the treatment into a rough draft screenplay, adding elements such as the Sith, the Death Star, and a protagonist named Annikin Starkiller. For the second draft, Lucas made heavy simplifications, and also introduced the young hero on a farm as Luke Skywalker. Anakin became Luke's father, a wise Jedi knight. "The Force" was also introduced as a supernatural power. The next draft removed the father character and replaced him with a substitute named Ben Kenobi, and in 1976 a fourth draft had been prepared for principal photography. The film was titled *Adventures of Luke Starkiller, as taken from the Journal of the Whills, Saga I: The Star Wars*. During production, Lucas changed Luke's name to Skywalker and altered the title to simply *The Star Wars* and finally *Star Wars*.

At that point, Lucas was not expecting the film to become part of a series. The fourth draft of the script underwent subtle changes that made it more satisfying as a self-contained film, ending with the destruction of the Empire itself by way of destroying the Death Star. However, Lucas *had* previously conceived of the film as the first in a series of adventures. Later, he realised the film would not in fact be the first in the sequence, but a film in the second trilogy in the saga. This is stated explicitly in George Lucas' preface to the 1994 reissue of *Splinter of the Mind's Eye*:

> It wasn't long after I began writing *Star Wars* that I realized the story was more than a single film could hold. As the saga of the Skywalkers and Jedi Knights unfolded, I began to see it as a tale that could take at least nine films to tell — three trilogies — and I realized, in making my way through the back story and after story, that I was really setting out to write the middle story.

The second draft contained a teaser for a never-made sequel about "The Princess of Ondos," and by the time of the third draft some months later Lucas had negotiated a contract that gave him rights to make two sequels. Not long after, Lucas met with author Alan Dean Foster, and hired him to write these two sequels as novels. The intention was that if *Star Wars* were successful, Lucas could adapt the novels into screenplays. He had also by that point developed a fairly elaborate backstory to aid his writing process.

When *Star Wars* proved successful, Lucas decided to use the film as the basis for an elaborate serial, although at one point he considered walking away from the series altogether. However, Lucas wanted to create an independent filmmaking center — what would become Skywalker Ranch — and saw an opportunity to use the series as a financing agent. Alan Dean Foster had already begun writing the first sequel novel, but Lucas decided to abandon his plan to adapt Foster's work; the book was released as *Splinter of the Mind's Eye* the following year. At first Lucas envisioned a series of films with no set number of entries, like the James Bond series. In an interview with *Rolling Stone* in August 1977, he said that he wanted his friends to each take a turn at directing the films and giving unique interpretations on the series. He also said that the backstory in which Darth Vader turns to the dark side, kills Luke's father and fights Ben Kenobi on a volcano as the Galactic Republic falls would make an excellent sequel.

Later that year, Lucas hired science fiction author Leigh Brackett to write *Star Wars II* with him. They held story conferences and, by late November 1977, Lucas had produced a handwritten treatment called *The Empire Strikes Back*. The treatment is very similar to the final film, except that Darth Vader does not reveal he is Luke's father. In the first draft that Brackett would write from this, Luke's father appears as a ghost to instruct Luke.

Brackett finished her first draft in early 1978; Lucas has said he was disappointed with it, but before he could discuss it with her, she died of cancer. With no writer available, Lucas had to write his next draft himself. It was this draft in which Lucas first made use of the "Episode" numbering for the films; *Empire Strikes Back* was listed as *Episode II*. As Michael Kaminski argues in *The Secret History of Star Wars*, the disappointment with the first draft probably made Lucas consider different directions in which to take the story. He made use of a new plot twist: Darth Vader claims to be Luke's father.

According to Lucas, he found this draft enjoyable to write, as opposed to the year-long struggles writing the first film, and quickly wrote two more drafts, both in April 1978. He also took the script to a darker extreme by having Han Solo imprisoned in carbonite and left in limbo.

This new story point of Darth Vader being Luke's father had drastic effects on the series. Michael Kaminski argues in his book that it is unlikely that the plot point had ever seriously been considered or even conceived of before 1978, and that the first film was clearly operating under an alternate storyline where Vader was separate from Luke's father; there is not a single reference to this plot point before 1978. After writing the second and third drafts of *Empire Strikes Back* in which the point was introduced, Lucas reviewed the new backstory he had created: Anakin Skywalker was Ben Kenobi's brilliant student and had a child named Luke, but was swayed to the dark side by Emperor Palpatine (who became a Sith and not simply a politician). Anakin battled Ben Kenobi on the site of a volcano and was wounded, but then resurrected as Darth Vader. Meanwhile Kenobi hid Luke on Tatooine while the Republic became the Empire and Vader systematically hunted down and killed the Jedi.

With this new backstory in place, Lucas decided that the series would be a trilogy, changing *Empire Strikes Back* from *Episode II* to *Episode V* in the next draft. Lawrence Kasdan, who had just completed writing *Raiders of the Lost Ark*, was then hired to write the next drafts, and was given additional input from director Irvin Kershner. Kasdan, Kershner, and producer Gary Kurtz saw the film as a more serious and adult film, which was helped by the new, darker storyline, and developed the series from the light adventure roots of the first film.

By the time he began writing *Episode VI* in 1981 (then titled *Revenge of the Jedi*), much had changed. Making *Empire Strikes Back* was stressful and costly, and Lucas' personal life was disintegrating. Burned out and not wanting to make any more *Star Wars* films, he vowed that he was done with the series in a May 1983 interview with *Time* magazine. Lucas' 1981 rough drafts had Darth Vader competing with the Emperor for possession of Luke — and in the second script, the "revised rough draft," Vader became a sympathetic character. Lawrence Kasdan was hired to take over once again and, in these final drafts, Vader was explicitly redeemed and finally unmasked. This change in character would provide a springboard to the "Tragedy of Darth Vader" storyline that underlies the prequels.

Prequel trilogy

After losing much of his fortune in a divorce settlement in 1987, Lucas had no desire to return to *Star Wars*, and had unofficially canceled his sequel trilogy by the time of *Return of the Jedi*. Nevertheless, the prequels, which were quite developed at this point, continued to fascinate him. After *Star Wars* became popular once again, in the wake of Dark Horse's comic book line and Timothy Zahn's trilogy of novels, Lucas saw that there was still a large audience. His children were older, and with the explosion of CGI technology he was now considering returning to directing. By 1993 it was announced, in *Variety* among other sources, that he would be making the prequels. He began outlining the story, now indicating the series would be a tragic one examining Anakin Skywalker's fall to the dark side. Lucas also began to change how the prequels would exist relative to the originals; at first they were supposed to be a "filling-in" of history, backstory, existing parallel or tangential to the originals, but now he saw that they could form the beginning of one long story that started with Anakin's childhood and ended with his death. This was the final step towards turning the film series into a "Saga".

In 1994, Lucas began writing the first screenplay titled *Episode I: The Beginning*. Following the release of that film, Lucas announced that he would also be directing the next two, and began working on *Episode II* at that time. The first draft of *Episode II* was completed just weeks before principal photography, and Lucas hired Jonathan Hales, a writer from *The Young Indiana Jones Chronicles*, to polish it. Unsure of a title, Lucas had jokingly called the film "Jar Jar's Great Adventure." In writing *The Empire Strikes Back*, Lucas initially decided that Lando Calrissian was a clone and came from a planet of clones which caused the "Clone Wars" mentioned by Obi-Wan Kenobi in *A New Hope*; he later came up with an alternate concept of an army of clone shocktroopers from a remote planet which attacked the Republic and were repelled by the Jedi. The basic elements of that backstory became the plot basis for *Episode II*, with the new wrinkle added that Palpatine secretly orchestrated the crisis.

Lucas began working on *Episode III* before *Attack of the Clones* was released, offering concept artists that the film would open with a montage of seven Clone War battles. As he reviewed the storyline that summer, however, he says he radically re-organized the plot. Michael Kaminski, in *The Secret History of Star Wars*, offers evidence that issues in Anakin's fall to the dark side prompted Lucas to make massive story changes, first revising the opening sequence to have Palpatine kidnapped and his apprentice, Count Dooku, murdered by Anakin as the first act in the latter's turn towards the dark side. After principal photography was complete in 2003, Lucas made even more massive changes in Anakin's character, re-writing his entire turn to the dark side; he would now turn primarily in a quest to save Padmé's life, rather than the previous version in which that reason was one of several, including that he genuinely believed that the Jedi were evil and plotting to take over the Republic. This fundamental re-write was accomplished both through editing the principal footage, and new and revised scenes filmed during pick-ups in 2004.

Lucas often exaggerated the amount of material he wrote for the series; much of it stemmed from the post–1978 period when the series grew into a phenomenon. Michael Kaminski explained that these exaggerations were both a publicity and security measure. Kaminski rationalized that since the series' story radically changed throughout the years, it was always Lucas' intention to change the original story retroactively because audiences would only view the material from his perspective.

Sequel trilogy

Main article: Star Wars sequel trilogy

The sequel trilogy was a reportedly planned trilogy of films (Episodes VII, VIII and IX) by Lucasfilm as a sequel to the original *Star Wars* trilogy (Episodes IV, V and VI) released between 1977 and 1983. While the similarly discussed *Star Wars* prequel trilogy (Episodes I, II and III) was ultimately released between 1999 and 2005, Lucasfilm and George Lucas have for many years denied plans of making a sequel trilogy, insisting that *Star Wars* is meant to be a six-part series.

Future releases

At a ShoWest convention in 2005, Lucas demonstrated new technology and stated that he planned to release the six films in a new 3-D film format, beginning with *A New Hope* in 2007. However, by January 2007, Lucasfilm stated on StarWars.com that "there are no definitive plans or dates for releasing the Star Wars saga in 3-D." At Celebration Europe in July 2007, Rick McCallum confirmed that Lucasfilm is "planning to take all six films and turn them into 3-D," but they are "waiting for the companies out there that are developing this technology to bring it down to a cost level that makes it worthwhile for everybody". In July 2008, Jeffrey Katzenberg, the CEO of Dreamworks Animations, revealed that Lucas plans to redo all six of the movies in 3D. In late September 2010, it was announced that *The Phantom Menace* will be theatrically re-released in 3-D during 2012. All six films will be re-released in order, with the 3-D conversion process taking at least a year to complete per film.

Lucas has hinted in the past that he will release future, more definitive editions of the six *Star Wars* films on a next-generation home-video format. There have been discussions that he will take this opportunity to make any final adjustments, changes, additions, and/or subtractions to his films for this final release. An altered clip from *The Phantom Menace* included in a featurette on the DVD release of *Revenge of the Sith* features a computer generated Yoda replacing the original puppet; animation director Rob Coleman stated that the clip had been created as test footage of Yoda prior to work on *Revenge of the Sith*. Lucasfilm Vice President of Marketing Jim Ward announced that Lucasfilm is likely to do more work on the films, stating "As the technology evolves and we get into a high-definition platform that is easily consumable by our customers, the situation is much better, but there will always be work to be done." At Chicago Comics and Entertainment Expo 2010, Steve Sansweet, Lucasfilm's Director of Fan Relations, revealed that "a very full set of all six movies on Blu-ray with lots of extra material" is being prepared for release. On August 14, 2010, George Lucas announced that all six *Star Wars* films will be released on Blu-ray Disc in the Fall of 2011.

Box office performance

Film	Release date	Box office revenue				Box office ranking	
		United States	Foreign	Worldwide	Adjusted for inflation (US)	All-time domestic	All-time worldwide
Star Wars Episode IV: A New Hope	May 25, 1977	$460,998,007	$314,400,000	$775,398,007	$1,416,050,800	#4	#30
Star Wars Episode V: The Empire Strikes Back	May 21, 1980	$290,475,067	$247,900,000	$538,375,067	$780,536,100	#38	#62
Star Wars Episode VI: Return of the Jedi	May 25, 1983	$309,306,177	$165,800,000	$475,106,177	$747,772,300	#29	#80
Original *Star Wars* trilogy		**$1,060,779,251**	**$728,100,000**	**$1,788,879,251**	**$2,944,359,200**		
Star Wars Episode I: The Phantom Menace	May 19, 1999	$431,088,301	$493,229,257	$924,317,558	$674,365,200	#7	#11
Star Wars Episode II: Attack of the Clones	May 16, 2002	$310,676,740	$338,721,588	$649,398,328	$425,074,300	#27	#42
Star Wars Episode III: Revenge of the Sith	May 19, 2005	$380,270,577	$468,728,238	$848,998,815	$471,630,400	#11	#20
Prequel *Star Wars* trilogy		**$1,122,035,618**	**$1,300,679,083**	**$2,422,714,701**	**$1,571,069,900**		
Star Wars: The Clone Wars	August 15, 2008	$35,161,554	$33,121,290	$68,282,844	$35,020,908	#1,557	—
Complete *Star Wars* film series		**$2,217,976,423**	**$2,061,900,373**	**$4,279,876,796**	**$4,384,857,465**		

Critical reaction

Film	Rotten Tomatoes		Metacritic
	Overall	Cream of the Crop	
Star Wars Episode IV: A New Hope	94% (63 reviews)	88% (17 reviews)	91 (13 reviews)
Star Wars Episode V: The Empire Strikes Back	97% (66 reviews)	88% (16 reviews)	78 (15 reviews)
Star Wars Episode VI: Return of the Jedi	78% (63 reviews)	76% (17 reviews)	52 (14 reviews)
Star Wars Episode I: The Phantom Menace	62% (158 reviews)	40% (47 reviews)	52 (35 reviews)
Star Wars Episode II: Attack of the Clones	66% (215 reviews)	40% (40 reviews)	53 (39 reviews)
Star Wars Episode III: Revenge of the Sith	80% (252 reviews)	67% (43 reviews)	68 (40 reviews)
Star Wars: The Clone Wars	19% (152 reviews)	15% (26 reviews)	35 (30 reviews)
Average	**71%**	**59%**	**61**

Academy Awards

The six films together were nominated for a total of 25 Academy Awards, of which they won ten. Three of these were Special Achievement Awards.

Award	Awards Won					
	IV: A New Hope	*V: The Empire Strikes Back*	*VI: Return of the Jedi*	*I: The Phantom Menace*	*II: Attack of the Clones*	*III: Revenge of the Sith*
Actor in a Supporting Role	Nomination (Alec Guinness)					
Art Direction-Set Decoration	Win	Nomination	Nomination			
Costume Design	Win					
Director	Nomination (George Lucas)					

Film Editing	Win					
Makeup						Nomination
Music (Original Score)	Win	Nomination	Nomination			
Picture	Nomination					
Screenplay – Original	Nomination					
Sound Editing			Nomination	Nomination		
Sound (Mixing)	Win	Win	Nomination	Nomination		
Visual Effects	Win			Nomination	Nomination	
Special Achievement Award	Win (Alien, Creature and Robot Voices)	Win (Visual Effects)	Win (Visual Effects)			

Expanded Universe

Main article: Star Wars Expanded Universe

The term *Expanded Universe* (*EU*) is an umbrella term for officially licensed *Star Wars* material outside of the six feature films. The material expands the stories told in the films, taking place anywhere from 25,000 years before *The Phantom Menace* to 140 years after *Return of the Jedi*. The first *Expanded Universe* story appeared in Marvel Comics' *Star Wars* #7 in January 1978 (the first six issues of the series having been an adaptation of the film), followed quickly by Alan Dean Foster's novel *Splinter of the Mind's Eye* the following month.

George Lucas retains artistic control over the *Star Wars* universe. For example, the death of central characters and similar changes in the status quo must first pass his screening before authors are given the go-ahead. In addition, Lucasfilm Licensing devotes efforts to ensure continuity between the works of various authors across companies. Elements of the Expanded Universe have been adopted by Lucas for use in the films, such as the name of capital planet Coruscant, which first appeared in Timothy Zahn's novel *Heir to the Empire* before being used in *The Phantom Menace*. Additionally, Lucas so liked the character Aayla Secura, who was introduced in Dark Horse Comics' *Star Wars* series, that he included her as a character in *Attack of the Clones*.

Lucas has played a large role in the production of various television projects, usually serving as storywriter or executive producer. *Star Wars* has had numerous radio adaptations. A radio adaptation of *A New Hope* was first broadcast on National Public Radio in 1981. The adaptation was written by science fiction author Brian Daley and directed by John Madden. It was followed by adaptations of *The Empire Strikes Back* in 1983 and *Return of the Jedi* in 1996. The adaptations included background material created by Lucas but not used in the films. Mark Hamill, Anthony Daniels, and Billy Dee Williams reprised their roles as Luke Skywalker, C-3PO, and Lando Calrissian, respectively, except in *Return of the Jedi* in which Luke was played by Joshua Fardon and Lando by Arye Gross. The series also used John Williams' original score from the films and Ben Burtt's original sound designs.

Other films

In addition to the two trilogies, several authorized films have been produced:

- *The Star Wars Holiday Special*, a 1978 two-hour television special, shown only once and never released on video. Notable for the introduction of Boba Fett.
- *Caravan of Courage: An Ewok Adventure*, a 1984 American made-for-TV film - released theatrically overseas.
- *Ewoks: The Battle for Endor*, a 1985 American made-for-TV film — released theatrically overseas.
- *The Great Heep*, a 1986 animated television special from the *Star Wars: Droids* TV series.
- *Star Wars: The Clone Wars*, a 2008 theatrical release that leads into the animated TV series of the same name.
- *Lego Star Wars: The Quest for R2-D2*, a 2009 official comedy spoof primarily based on *The Clone Wars* film.

Animated series

Following the success of the *Star Wars* films and their subsequent merchandising, several animated television series have been created for the younger fan base:

- *Star Wars: Droids*, also known as *Droids*, which premiered in September 1985, focused on the travels of R2-D2 and C-3P0 as they shift through various different owners/masters, and vaguely fills in the gaps between the events of *Star Wars Episode III: Revenge of the Sith* and *Star Wars Episode IV: A New Hope*.
- *Star Wars: Ewoks* and colloquially as *The Ewoks*, was simultaneously released in September 1985 and focused on the adventures of Wicket and various other recognizable Ewok characters from the original trilogy in the years leading up to *Star Wars Episode VI: Return of the Jedi*.
- *Star Wars: Clone Wars* cartoon micro-series created by Genndy Tartakovsky, which aired on Cartoon Network from November 2003 to March 2005.
- *Star Wars: The Clone Wars* animated series continuation of the animated movie of the same name, which has been airing on Cartoon Network since October 2008.
- Untitled *Star Wars* Animated Series: an animated comedy series written by Brendan Hay, who is a writer for the comedy news show *The Daily Show*, and with creative consulting from the co-creators of *Robot Chicken*: Seth Green and Matthew Senreich. The series will take place during the original trilogy and the setting will be remote from the front line of war.

Literature

Main articles: List of Star Wars books and List of Star Wars comic books

Star Wars-based fiction predates the release of the first film, with the 1976 novelization of *Star Wars* (ghost-written by Alan Dean Foster and credited to Lucas). Foster's 1978 novel, *Splinter of the Mind's Eye*, was the first Expanded Universe work to be released. In addition to filling in the time between *A New Hope* and *The Empire Strikes Back*, this additional content greatly expanded the *Star Wars* timeline before and after the film series. *Star Wars* fiction flourished during the time of the original trilogy (1977–1983) but slowed to a trickle afterwards. In 1992, however, Timothy Zahn's *Thrawn trilogy* debuted, sparking a new interest in the *Star Wars* universe. Since then, several hundred tie-in novels have been published by Bantam and Del Rey. A similar resurgence in the Expanded Universe occurred in 1996 with the Steve Perry novel *Shadows of the Empire*, set in between *The Empire Strikes Back* and *Return of the Jedi*, and accompanying video game and comic book series.

LucasBooks radically changed the face of the *Star Wars* universe with the introduction of the *New Jedi Order* series, which takes place some 20 years after *Return of the Jedi* and stars a host of new characters alongside series originals. For younger audiences, three series have been introduced. The *Jedi Apprentice* series follows the adventures of Qui-Gon Jinn and his apprentice Obi-Wan Kenobi prior to *The Phantom Menace*. The *Jedi Quest* series follows the adventures of Obi-Wan and his apprentice Anakin Skywalker in between *The Phantom Menace* and *Attack of the Clones*. *The Last of the Jedi* series follows the adventures of Obi-Wan and another surviving Jedi almost immediately following *Revenge of the Sith*.

Marvel Comics published *Star Wars* comic book series and adaptations from 1977 to 1986. A wide variety of creators worked on this series, including Roy Thomas, Archie Goodwin, Howard Chaykin, Al Williamson, Carmine Infantino, Gene Day, Walt Simonson, Michael Golden, Chris Claremont, Whilce Portacio, Jo Duffy, and Ron Frenz. They also published a *Star Wars* newspaper strip by Russ Manning, Steve Gerber, and Archie Goodwin, the latter under a pseudonym. In the late 1980s, Marvel announced it would publish a new *Star Wars* comic by Tom Veitch and Cam Kennedy. However, in December 1991, Dark Horse Comics acquired the *Star Wars* license and used it to launch a number of ambitious sequels to the original trilogy instead, including the popular *Dark Empire* stories. They have since gone on to publish a large number of original adventures set in the *Star Wars* universe. There have also been parody comics, including *Tag and Bink*.

Games

Main articles: Star Wars computer and video games, List of Star Wars video games, and Star Wars Trading Cards

Since 1982, dozens of video games have been published bearing the *Star Wars* name, beginning with *Star Wars: The Empire Strikes Back* published for the Atari 2600 by Parker Brothers. Since then, *Star Wars* has opened the way to a myriad of space-flight simulation games, first-person shooter games, roleplaying games, RTS games, and others. Two different official tabletop role-playing games have been developed for the *Star Wars* universe: a version by West End Games in the 1980s and 1990s, and one by Wizards of the Coast in the 2000s. The best-selling games so far are the *Lego Star Wars* and the *Battlefront* series, with 12 million and 10 million units respectively. *Star Wars: Knights of the Old Republic* is also an extremely well-known game.

The latest games released are *Lego Star Wars: The Complete Saga*, *Star Wars: The Force Unleashed* and *Star Wars: The Force Unleashed II*, for the PS3, PSP, PS2, Xbox 360, Nintendo DS and Wii. While *The Complete Saga* focuses on all six episodes of the series, *The Force Unleashed*, of the same name of the multimedia project which it is a part of, takes place in the largely unexplored time period between *Star Wars Episode III: Revenge of the Sith* and *Star Wars Episode IV: A New Hope* and casts players as Darth Vader's "secret apprentice" hunting down the remaining Jedi. The game features a new game engine, and was released on September 16, 2008 in the United States. There are two more titles based on the Clone Wars which were released in November 2008 for the Nintendo DS (*Star Wars: The Clone Wars – Jedi Alliance*) and Wii (*Star Wars: The Clone Wars – Lightsaber Duels*).

Star Wars trading cards have been published since the first 'blue' series, by Topps, in 1977. Dozens of series have been produced, with Topps being the licensed creator in the United States. Some of the card series are of film stills, while others are original art. Many of the cards have become highly collectible with some very rare "promos", such as the 1993 Galaxy Series II "floating Yoda" P3 card often commanding US$1000 or more. While most "base" or "common card" sets are plentiful, many "insert" or "chase cards" are very rare.

The board game Risk has been adapted to the series in two editions by Hasbro: Risk Star Wars: The Original Trilogy Edition (2006) and Risk Star Wars: Clone Wars Edition (2005).

Fan works

Main article: Star Wars fan films

The *Star Wars* saga has inspired many fans to create their own non-canon material set in the *Star Wars* galaxy. In recent years, this has ranged from writing fan-fiction to creating fan films. In 2002, Lucasfilm sponsored the first annual Official Star Wars Fan Film Awards, officially recognizing filmmakers and the genre. Because of concerns over potential copyright and trademark issues, however, the contest was initially open only to parodies, mockumentaries, and documentaries.

Fan-fiction films set in the *Star Wars* universe were originally ineligible, but in 2007 Lucasfilm changed the submission standards to allow in-universe fiction entries.

While many fan films have used elements from the licensed Expanded Universe to tell their story, they are not considered an official part of the *Star Wars* canon. However, the lead character from the *Pink Five* series was incorporated into Timothy Zahn's 2007 novel *Allegiance*, marking the first time a fan-created *Star Wars* character has ever crossed into the official canon. Lucasfilm, for the most part, has allowed but not endorsed the creation of these derivative fan-fiction works, so long as no such work attempts to make a profit from or tarnish the *Star Wars* franchise in any way.

Attractions

In 1986, George Lucas established a partnership with the Walt Disney Company's Walt Disney Imagineering division to create *Star Tours*, an attraction that later opened at Disneyland in 1987. The attraction also had subsequent incarnations at other Disney parks worldwide, with the exception of Hong Kong Disneyland.

The original ride at Disneyland

The attractions at Disneyland and Disney's Hollywood Studios closed on July 27, 2010 and September 7, 2010 respectively, in order to allow the rides to be converted into the upcoming *Star Tours: The Adventures Continue* attraction.

Legacy

Main article: Cultural impact of Star Wars

The *Star Wars* saga has had a significant impact on modern American pop culture. Both the films and characters have been parodied in numerous films and television. Notable film parodies of *Star Wars* include *Hardware Wars*, a 13 minute 1977 spoof which Lucas has called his favorite Star Wars parody, and *Spaceballs*, a feature film by Mel Brooks which featured effects done by Lucas' Industrial Light & Magic. Lucasfilm itself made two mockumentaries: *Return of the Ewok* (1982), about Warwick Davis, who portrayed Wicket W. Warrick in *Return of the Jedi*; and *R2-D2: Beneath the Dome* (2002), which depicts R2-D2's "life story". There have also been many songs based on, and in, the *Star Wars* universe. "Weird Al" Yankovic recorded two parodies: "Yoda", a parody of "Lola" by The Kinks; and "The Saga Begins", a parody of Don McLean's song "American Pie" that retells of *The Phantom Menace* from Obi-Wan Kenobi's perspective.* In television, the creators of the *Robot Chicken* series has produced three television specials satirizing the *Star Wars* films. Also the creators of the *Family Guy* series have also produced three Star Wars specials titled Blue Harvest, Something, Something,

Something, Dark Side, and It's a Trap!.

When Ronald Reagan proposed the Strategic Defense Initiative (SDI), a system of lasers and missiles meant to intercept incoming ICBMs, the plan was quickly labeled "Star Wars," implying that it was science fiction and linking it to Ronald Reagan's acting career. According to Frances FitzGerald, Reagan was annoyed by this, but Assistant Secretary of Defense Richard Perle told colleagues that he "thought the name was not so bad."; "'Why not?' he said. 'It's a good movie. Besides, the good guys won.'" This gained further resonance when Reagan described the Soviet Union as an "Evil empire".

See also

- Architecture of Star Wars
- Dates in Star Wars
- *Empire of Dreams: The Story of the Star Wars Trilogy*
- List of Star Wars creatures
- List of Star Wars weapons
- Physics and Star Wars
- Star Wars canon
- Star Wars Day
- *The Story of Star Wars*
- Jedi census phenomenon
- Jediism
- Star Wars music

References

- Arnold, Alan (1980). *Once Upon a Galaxy: A Journal of the Making of The Empire Strikes Back* [1]. Ballantine Books. ISBN 0345290755
- Bouzereau, Laurent (1997). *The Annotated Screenplays* [2]. Del Rey. ISBN 0345409817
- Kaminski, Michael (2007). "The Secret History of Star Wars" [3]
- Kaminski, Michael (2008). "The Secret History of Star Wars" [3]. Retrieved 2008-05-21
- Rinzler, J.W. (2007). *The Making of Star Wars: The Definitive Story Behind the Original Film (Star Wars)* [4]. Del Rey. ISBN 0345494768
- Rinzler, Jonathan (2005). *The Making of Star Wars, Episode III - Revenge of the Sith* [5]. Del Rey. ISBN 0345431391.

Further reading

- Star Wars, religion, and philosophy
  - Bortolin, Matthew (2005-04-25). *The Dharma of Star Wars* [6]. Wisdom Publications. ISBN 0861714970.
  - Decker, Kevin S. (2005-03-10). *Star Wars and Philosophy* [7]. Open Court. ISBN 0812695836.
  - Porter, John M. (2003-01-31). *The Tao of Star Wars* [8]. Humanics Trade Group. ISBN 0893343854.
  - Snodgrass, Jon (2004-09-13). *Peace Knights of the Soul* [9]. InnerCircle Publishing. ISBN 0975521470.

- Staub, Dick (2005-03-25). *Christian Wisdom of the Jedi Masters* [10]. Jossey-Bass. ISBN 0787978949.
- Joseph Campbell's influence on Star Wars
  - Campbell, Joseph (1991-06-01). *The Power of Myth* [11]. Anchor. ISBN 0385418868.
  - Henderson, Mary (1997-11-03). *Star Wars: The Magic of Myth* [12]. Bantam. ISBN 0553102060.
  - Larsen, Stephen (2002-04-01). *Joseph Campbell: A Fire in the Mind* [13]. Inner Traditions. ISBN 0892818735.

External links

- The Official *Star Wars* Website [14]
- Star Wars [15] at the Open Directory Project
- Wookieepedia: The *Star Wars* Wiki – A wiki devoted to *Star Wars*
- *Star Wars* Origins: How did George Lucas create *Star Wars*? [16]

Jack Ryan

Jack Ryan (Tom Clancy)

First appearance	*The Hunt for Red October* (1984)
Created by	Tom Clancy
Portrayed by	Alec Baldwin, Harrison Ford, Ben Affleck
Gender	Male
Occupation	US President, National Security Advisor, CIA Deputy Director of Central Intelligence, USMC Second Lieutenant
Spouse(s)	Caroline "Cathy" M. Ryan (née Muller)
Children	Olivia "Sally" Ryan, Jack Ryan Jr., Kathleen "Katie" Ryan, Kyle Ryan
Religion	Catholic

Jack Ryan is a fictional character created by Tom Clancy who appears in many of his novels.

Biography

Backstory

Ryan's background is established in *Patriot Games and Red Rabbit*. Born in 1950, he is the son of Emmet William Ryan (1922–1974), a police homicide lieutenant and World War II veteran. The elder Ryan had served with the U.S. Army's 101st Airborne Division at the Battle of the Bulge. His mother, Catherine Burke Ryan, (1923–1974) was a nurse.

After graduating from Loyola High School in Towson, Maryland, Ryan attended Boston College, graduating with a Bachelor of Arts degree in Economics (with a strong minor in history) and a commission as a Second Lieutenant in the United States Marine Corps (via NROTC). While waiting for the Marine Corps to assign him somewhere, he passed the Certified Public Accountant exam.

After officer training at Quantico, he eventually went on to serve as a platoon commander. However, his military career was cut short at the age of 23 when his platoon's helicopter, a CH-46 Sea Knight, crashed during a NATO exercise over the Greek island of Crete. Ryan's back was badly injured in the crash. Navy surgeons at the National Naval Medical Center in Bethesda made inadequate repairs to his back. This led to a lengthy recovery process (during which he nearly became addicted to pain medications) after which, complete with a permanent disability and wearing a back brace, he left the Marine Corps. He passed his stock broker's exam and took a position with the Baltimore office of the Wall Street investment firm Merrill Lynch.

(The movie adaptation of *The Hunt for Red October* tells Ryan's story differently: Admiral Joshua Painter states that he attended the United States Naval Academy and that in the "summer of his third year, he went down in a chopper accident. Bad. Pilot and crew killed. That kid spent 10 months in traction and another year learning to walk again. He did his fourth year from the hospital." The film is inconsistent with the novels, which are generally considered canonical, not least in their depiction of Ryan's first meeting with Admiral James Greer.)

His parents died in a plane crash at Chicago's Midway Airport only 19 months after his crash in Crete. He developed a fear of flying that persisted for years.

Civilian career

Ryan's story starts in *Patriot Games* and continues in *Red Rabbit*. While managing clients' portfolios, he began to invest his own money, banking on a tip he had received from an uncle about the workers' takeover of the Chicago and North Western Railroad, making approximately $6 million off his $100,000 initial investment. He did so well that a senior VP of Merrill Lynch, Joe Muller, came to Baltimore to have dinner with him, with the objective of inviting him to the New York City headquarters. Also present is Muller's daughter Caroline, nicknamed Cathy, then a senior medical student at the Johns Hopkins University School of Medicine. They immediately fall in love and get engaged. One night, while having dinner with his fiancée, Ryan throws out his back. Cathy takes him directly to Doctor Stanley Rabinowitz, professor of neurosurgery at Johns Hopkins, to be evaluated. Rabinowitz later operates on Ryan's back and cures his chronic pain in relatively short order. Ryan subsequently persuades the government to terminate his disability checks. Cathy later becomes an ophthalmic surgeon at the Wilmer Eye Institute of Johns Hopkins University School of Medicine and a Professor of Surgery at Johns Hopkins.

After establishing a net worth of $8 million, Ryan left the firm after four years and enrolled at Georgetown University for his doctorate courses in history. He does a brief stint at the Center for Strategic and International Studies, then accepts a position at the U.S. Naval Academy in Annapolis, Maryland as a civilian professor of history.

First CIA work

Following a recommendation of Father Tim O'Riley, PhD, S.J., (a Georgetown University professor) to a CIA contact, Ryan is asked to work as an outside consultant for the Agency, although officially employed by MITRE Corporation. He agrees and spends several months at Langley, Virginia, where he writes a paper entitled *"Agents and Agencies"*, in which he maintains that state-sponsored terrorism is an act of war. He also invents the canary trap, a method for exposing an information leak, which involves giving different versions of a sensitive document to each of a group of suspects and seeing which version gets leaked. By making sure that each copy of the document differs slightly in its wording, if any copy is leaked then it is possible to determine the identity of the informant.

Both of these accomplishments come to the attention of U.S. Navy Vice Admiral James Greer, the Deputy Director (Intelligence) at the CIA. The expertise of Ryan's report, plus the application, persuades Admiral Greer to offer him a permanent job in the CIA, but Ryan turns it down.

While Ryan is still teaching at the Naval Academy, he and his family (wife and daughter Sally) take a trip to London for research and vacationing. After spending the day sifting through Royal Navy archives doing research for a book on the British naval war in the Indian Ocean during World War II, Ryan walks to meet his family at a London park. As he joins them, members of the Ulster Liberation Army, an ultra-violent Maoist offshoot of the Marxist IRA, headed by a man named Kevin O'Donnell, attack a car containing the Prince of Wales and his family right in front of Ryan and his wife and daughter. Ryan becomes wounded while intervening the attack and foils their plan, killing one of the gunmen and capturing another.

Sean Miller, the man he captured, vows revenge on Ryan and his family. But since he is going to Albany Prison on the Isle of Wight, the threat doesn't seem serious. After being invested as a Knight Commander of the Royal Victorian Order by the Queen, Ryan returns to the U.S. and the Academy. When O'Donnell and the ULA spring Miller on his way to Albany Prison (killing both police officers and civilians in the process), Ryan and his family become the target of their revenge—particularly Miller's.

CIA career

In *Patriot Games*, Greer comes to Ryan and asks him to return to join the CIA permanently as an analyst to help track down the terrorists. He declines initially, only to accept it later after a failed attack on himself and his family by the ULA severely injures his wife and daughter. Later, while Ryan hosts the Prince and Princess of Wales at his home in Maryland, the ULA make a second attack on the Ryans, which is foiled by Jack, the Prince, and Commander Robert Jackson, USN. Following the incident and arrest of the ULA, he is re-assigned to London as a member of a liaison group to the British Secret Intelligence Service.

In *Red Rabbit*, Ryan's assignment to London focuses on a daring mission to assist the defection of a KGB communications-center officer who has discovered that KGB director Yuri Andropov had ordered the assassination attempt on Pope John Paul II. Although Ryan and a small team of British agents helps the "Rabbit" and his family get to the West, they fail to prevent the attack on the Pope. Nevertheless, "Rabbit's" defection proves to be a major coup for both American and British intelligence. Ryan soon afterward suggests a non-military strategy to help hasten the USSR's collapse.

In *The Hunt for Red October*, Captain First Rank Marko Ramius, the Soviet Navy's top submarine commander, takes command of the *Красный Октябрь* (*Red October*), the newest Typhoon class submarine, which he plans to defect with. Ryan recognizes this and works to welcome him to the United States, eventually succeeding.

In *The Cardinal of the Kremlin*, Ryan is reassigned to Langley. He becomes Greer's assistant with the official title of Special Assistant to the Deputy Director for Intelligence. Greer is grooming the rising analyst for bigger and better positions, maybe even his own job when the veteran spy finally retired. Ryan is dispatched to Moscow as part of the American strategic nuclear weapons reduction negotiation team. There he meets Sergey Golovko, a rising star in the KGB hierarchy, and eventually becomes entangled in a complex web related to both the race to develop "Star Wars" space-based defensive technology and engineer another defection, this time compromising the KGB director to save the CIA's highest informant in the USSR, Agent CARDINAL, better known as Colonel Misha Filitov. Although they initially meet as adversaries—literally at gunpoint—Golovko respects him as a worthy adversary and in later books becomes friends with Ryan, whom he calls "Ivan Emmetovich," giving him a Russian-style patronymic based on his father's name, Emmet.

In *Clear and Present Danger*, Ryan is promoted to acting DDI when Greer is hospitalized with cancer. Despite this he is kept out of the loop on a highly covert and illegal CIA operation approved by corrupt National Security Advisor Admiral Cutter. This operation targets Colombian drug lords using military assets, in what is usually considered a law enforcement area. Ryan eventually works with the FBI to rescue a small group of American soldiers cut off in the Colombian wilderness, which forces him to miss Greer's funeral. Around this time Ryan also runs afoul of Elizabeth Elliott, international affairs advisor to then presidential candidate Governor of Ohio J. Robert Fowler, and a former professor of Cathy Ryan's.

In *The Sum of All Fears*, Ryan reaches his highest post at the CIA; Deputy Director of Central Intelligence. His career is placed in jeopardy when Fowler becomes President and Elizabeth Elliott becomes both National Security Advisor and Fowler's lover/manipulator. They not only deny Ryan any credit for an innovative Middle East peace plan, but also panic when terrorists detonate a nuclear bomb in Denver during the Super Bowl and nearly plunge the world into a Soviet-American nuclear war. Ryan defuses the nuclear crisis by commandeering the Washington-Moscow hot line and convincing the Soviet premier (through his friend Golovko) that the crisis is a setup. He then refuses to confirm Fowler's order to launch a nuclear missile at Qom (thus preventing the attack), where the Iranian Ayatollah lived. The crisis effectively ends Fowler's administration and, on this note, Ryan retires from the CIA. (The movie version again departs from the printed version, by presenting a younger, unmarried Ryan and a resurrected Greer-like Marcus Cabot. These changes are typical of attempts to "reboot" a franchise.)

Presidency

In *Debt of Honor*, Ryan returns to government service to deal with a second war between Japan and the United States. For a brief time Ryan is the National Security Advisor, but when Vice President Ed Kealty is forced to resign after a sex scandal, President Roger Durling taps him for the job. Ryan accepts the Office of Vice President on the condition that it is only until the end of Durling's current term. He sees this as a way of ending his public life. Moments after he is confirmed by Congress, a Japanese airline pilot deliberately crashes his 747 into the Capitol during a joint session of Congress, killing most of the people inside, decapitating the U.S. government and elevating Ryan to the Presidency.

The reluctant yet determined Ryan Administration emerges in *Executive Orders* as Ryan slowly rebuilds the government. He is faced with political trickery by Ed Kealty, and a deadly plague initiated by the newly formed United Islamic Republic, resulting in two major military conflicts far from American shores.

In *The Bear and the Dragon*, it is established that Ryan has completed Durling's term as President and has campaigned for—and won—the next Presidential election. He retains most of his emergency Cabinet and has Robby Jackson as Vice-President.

Ryan has to deal with the attempted assassination of Golovko, head of the SVR (formerly the KGB). This turns out to be an attempt to sow confusion in the Russian government because of China's designs to annex Eastern Siberia, where geologists had recently discovered a large amount of oil and gold. These events eventually lead to the inclusion of Russia into NATO and the assistance of US forces in the Sino-Russian War. When the Chinese begin losing the war, U.S. forces begin to target their strategic assets. A SSN sinks a Chinese SSBN, which causes the Chinese Politburo to panic and to increase the readiness of their 12 land-based ICBMs. US forces do not have the ability to destroy the silos, as they could only use deep penetrating bombs, which had all been used to destroy Chinese bridges to disrupt the PLA's logistical support. This causes the U.S. and Russia to send a joint RAINBOW and Spetsnaz team to destroy the silos. They destroy 11 of the 12 ICBMs but one of them manages to launch. The warhead heads towards Washington, DC; and with Ryan taking a command initiative at an Aegis missile cruiser, the ICBM is intercepted by ABM's from the USS *Gettysburg*. With the looming defeat of the PLA in Siberia, which they were about to learn about via live UAV broadcasts from the CIA through the Internet, student demonstrators in Beijing raid the Politburo, which causes a conservative minister to take control and arrest the perpetrators of the war in Siberia and surrender to the US and Russia.

Following this, Ryan apparently completes his term as president and refuses to run for a second elected term. Robby Jackson thus campaigns to become the first African American president, but is assassinated on a trip to the South, which enables Ed Kealty to become the next President. (It is also possible from what Jack Ryan Jr. says in *Teeth of the Tiger* that Jack Sr. resigned, feeling he has done what he needed to as President, and encouraged Robby Jackson to run for the Presidency.) Before Ryan actually leaves office, he creates "The Campus," a secret counter-terrorism organization that fronts as Hendley Associates, a financial trading company. He also writes presidential pardons out to all of its members, with the assistance of his Attorney General Pat Martin.

In his retirement, Ryan is living easy with a comfortable net worth of over $80 million. He is currently working on two versions of his memoirs, one for immediate release, and another detailing his career at CIA, to be published posthumously.

Ryan Doctrine

At the end of *Executive Orders*, Ryan, in the tradition of Presidents Monroe, Truman, Carter and Reagan, issues a foreign policy doctrine which largely defines his administration's international perspective. The Ryan Doctrine states that the United States will no longer tolerate attacks on "our territory, our possessions, or our citizens," and adds that whoever orders such an attack will be held accountable by the United States.

This statement comes soon after the Ebola attack on the United States ordered by Mahmoud Haji Daryaei, the dictator of the new United Islamic Republic. Ryan announces the new doctrine on the same day that Daryaei is killed by two stealth bombers, on Ryan's orders. Therefore, the Ryan Doctrine apparently supersedes the executive order put in place by President Ford, which forbids the assassination of foreign heads of state. Ryan, however, believes it is a more ethical alternative than all-out war, since it punishes the person responsible for the attack instead of the people he rules.

Within the books the Ryan Doctrine is not officially invoked after Daryaei's death (although Ryan threatens to use it on the Chinese leadership in *The Bear and the Dragon*, should anything happen to American citizens living in the People's Republic of China as a consequence of the Siberian War).

Novels

The first book written to feature Jack Ryan was *The Hunt for Red October*.

By publication date

Books in the order in which they were written:

- *The Hunt for Red October* (1984)
- *Patriot Games* (1987)
- *The Cardinal of the Kremlin* (1988)
- *Clear and Present Danger* (1989)
- *The Sum of All Fears* (1991)

- *Without Remorse* (1993)
- *Debt of Honor* (1994)
- *Executive Orders* (1996)
- *Rainbow Six* (1998)
- *The Bear and the Dragon* (2000)
- *Red Rabbit* (2002)
- *The Teeth of the Tiger* (2003)
- *Dead or Alive* (2010)

Chronological order

In the order in which they occur in the storyline (and when they occur):

- *Without Remorse* (1970)
- *Patriot Games* (1981, based on a reference to Ryan's age, which is 31 at the beginning of the novel. This roughly fits with a reference to the Princess of Wales expecting a baby - in reality, Prince William was born in summer 1982)
- *Red Rabbit* (circa spring of 1982, based on references to living Leonid Brezhnev and Mikhail Suslov, both of whom died in 1982, as well as Jack Ryan Jr.'s age in the novel, 6 months)
- *The Hunt for Red October* (1984)
- *The Cardinal of the Kremlin* (1987)

Starting with the following novel, the series becomes distinctly different from real history as noted below.

- *Clear and Present Danger* (1988) - "The President" is referred to as distinct from Ronald Reagan, but events in Cardinal of the Kremlin are referred to as having concluded less than a year before the start of the novel, which takes place during an election year. Setting "Cardinal of the Kremlin" in 1991 misplaces the state of US-Soviet relations, and 1984 is before the War on Drugs warranted the attention given in "Clear and Present Danger". Ryan, as acting DDI is tasked with presenting a security briefing to the Presidential candidate, which included a copy of the 1984 election briefing. The only logical date is therefore 1988. However, The Sum of All Fears directly refers to George H. W. Bush and implies there to be a separate, still unnamed President before J. Robert Fowler.
- *The Sum of All Fears* (1991–92) – Israel partially cedes sovereignty over Jerusalem to the Vatican and Saudi Arabia, and the city becomes a UN protectorate policed by Swiss Guards. Residents of Jerusalem can choose between either Vatican, Israeli or Islamic judicial law. Denver is devastated by a terrorist nuclear explosion. The book occurs after the Persian Gulf War and before the dissolution of the Soviet Union. While it is implied that both events occur at the same time in the Ryanverse as in actual history, 1991, this conflicts with the terrorist attack on Denver, which occurs while the city is hosting the Super Bowl in the novel. The 1991 Super Bowl had already been played, meaning the terrorist attack would have occurred in early 1992, after the Soviet Union

actually fell.

- *Debt of Honor* (1995–96) – The U.S. and Russia destroy all of their ballistic missiles. After crippling the US economy and becoming a nuclear power, Japan invades and takes the Marianas Islands; the US and Japan fight a brief war, which the Japanese lose (they are subsequently denuclearized); an embittered Japanese pilot and proponent of the war crashes a 747 into the US Capitol Building immediately after Ryan's confirmation vote for the Vice President, killing most of the House and Senate, the President, all nine Supreme Court justices, the senior military establishment (including the JCS), and most of the Cabinet; Ryan is left in charge of a gutted government. The end of the book occurs shortly after the New Hampshire primary, which shows that the novel takes place during the 1996 election. Of interest, but not crucial to the plot of this or further books is that North and South Korea were said to be unified at some point between The Sum of All Fears and this book.
- *Executive Orders* (1996) – Saddam Hussein is assassinated; Iran and Iraq merge forming the United Islamic Republic; the UIR launches a biological attack on the U.S. using the Ebola virus; the US launches the Second Persian Gulf War against the UIR and defeats them; the Ayatollah is killed in a smart-bomb attack by the US.
- *Rainbow Six* (Takes place between Executive Orders and The Bear and the Dragon)(although events seem to be based on the Sydney Olympics held in 2000) RAINBOW - an elite counter-terrorist force - is created and engages terrorists across Europe. Ecoterrorists plan to create a genetically-enhanced virus based on Ebola and cancer cells, which they plan to use to wipe out much of the world's population.
- *The Bear and the Dragon* (2000) – Russia is admitted to NATO; China and Russia fight a major war, in which the US intervenes on its NATO ally's side. It implies that the British Prime Minister is Tony Blair.
- *The Teeth of the Tiger* (2005, based on the age of Jack Ryan Jr.) The U.S. is now engaged in a global war on terrorism, in response to the September 11th attacks which occurred in the Ryanverse as they did in the real world. It is mentioned that the wars in Afghanistan and Iraq occurred in the Ryanverse continuity, and that the Jerusalem Treaty signed in *The Sum of All Fears* has failed as Israelis and Palestinians went back to fighting each other.

Presidents

A total of five presidents are explicitly shown in the series (although *Red Rabbit* takes place during the Reagan Administration, Reagan does not make an appearance as a character):

- The unnamed man referred to only as "the President," first introduced in *The Hunt for Red October*; he remains in office through *The Cardinal of the Kremlin*, and *Clear and Present Danger*. At the end of the last novel, he runs for reelection and is defeated.
- **J. Robert Fowler,** former governor of Ohio, who defeats the incumbent at the end of *Clear and Present Danger* and is in office during *The Sum of All Fears*. After his failure to handle the Denver

crisis nearly results in nuclear war, he resigns from office at the end of the novel.

- **Roger Durling,** Fowler's vice-president, former governor of California and a Vietnam veteran with service in the 82nd Airborne Division. Durling replaces Fowler when the latter resigns, and is the President in *Debt of Honor*, completing Fowler's term as President. At the end of the novel, he is killed along with most of the government when a Japanese jetliner is crashed into the Capitol Building.
- **John Patrick Ryan** is confirmed as Durling's new vice-president at the end of *Debt of Honor*, and is sworn in as President when Durling is murdered on the same day. His claim to the presidency is contested by Durling's former VP Edward Kealty, but the courts eventually rule in Ryan's favor. He remains in office in *Executive Orders*, *Rainbow Six* (though he never appears) and *The Bear and the Dragon*.
- **Robert Jefferson "Robby" Jackson** succeeded Ryan as President of the United States after Ryan retired (as described in *The Teeth of the Tiger*), with Ryan believing he could leave the country in Robby's capable hands. After serving out the remainder of Ryan's term, Robby campaigned for his own re-election. While travelling in Mississippi, however, Jackson was shot and subsequently assassinated by a 67-year-old man who was a member of the Ku Klux Klan; Duane Farmer. Farmer was taken alive and swiftly executed for his crimes.
- President Edward Kealty: Durling's former vice-president, replaced by Jack Ryan after a sex scandal. During *Executive Orders*, he tries to steal the presidency from Ryan by claiming that he never actually resigned, but those allegations are tossed out by U.S. courts. After Ryan leaves office and Jackson is assassinated, Kealty is elected President in his own right, a position he holds in *The Teeth of the Tiger* though he is never seen..

It should be noted that in later books there are nevertheless multiple references to both the Reagan Presidency and the George H.W. Bush Presidency as if they had happened.

In films

Four movies have been produced based on Clancy novels featuring Jack Ryan, starring three different actors as Ryan:

<table>
<tr><th rowspan="2">Character</th><th colspan="4">Film</th></tr>
<tr><th>The Hunt for Red October (1990)</th><th>Patriot Games (1992)</th><th>Clear and Present Danger (1994)</th><th>The Sum of All Fears (2002)</th></tr>
<tr><td>Jack Ryan</td><td>Alec Baldwin</td><td colspan="2">Harrison Ford</td><td>Ben Affleck</td></tr>
<tr><td>James Greer</td><td colspan="3">James Earl Jones</td><td></td></tr>
<tr><td>Caroline Ryan</td><td>Gates McFadden</td><td colspan="2">Anne Archer</td><td>Bridget Moynahan</td></tr>
<tr><td>Sally Ryan</td><td>Louise Borras</td><td colspan="2">Thora Birch</td><td></td></tr>
<tr><td>John Clark</td><td colspan="2"></td><td>Willem Dafoe</td><td>Liev Schreiber</td></tr>
<tr><td>William Cabot</td><td colspan="3"></td><td>Morgan Freeman</td></tr>
</table>

In the novels, *Patriot Games* occurs before *The Hunt for Red October*, though the order was reversed in the film versions.

The Sum of All Fears is not part of the Baldwin/Ford series, but rather an intended reboot of the franchise, and therefore departs significantly from the chronology of the novels. It takes place in 2002 whereas the novel takes place in 1991/1992.

On March 18, 2008, *Variety* reported that Sam Raimi and Paramount Pictures were in negotiations to have Raimi direct the (second) franchise reboot, with intentions of having him spearheading multiple sequels. At the time, Tom Clancy was writing a new novel. Paramount had not decided to use this new story, or create an original story for the Jack Ryan reboot.[*citation needed*]

It was reported in October 2009, by the *Hollywood.com* official website and *cinemablend.com*, that Chris Pine was in talks to play Jack Ryan in a new reboot of the franchise.

Video games

Many video games based on the series have been made, some based on the novels, some on the films, some on the spin-offs.

- *The Hunt for Red October* (1987)

  The 1987 video game is based on the book

- *The Hunt for Red October* (1990)

  The 1990 video game is based on the film

- *The Sum of All Fears* (2002)

  The 2002 video game is based on the film

In addition there is the *Rainbow Six* video game universe, see Tom Clancy's Rainbow Six

See also

- John Clark
- Domingo Chavez
- Jack Ryan Jr.
- List of fictional U.S. Presidents

References

- Clancy, Tom (1984). *Hunt for Red October, The*. Naval Institute Press. ISBN 0-8702-1285-0.
- Clancy, Tom (1987). *Patriot Games*. G.P. Putnam & Son. ISBN 0-3991-3241-4.
- Clancy, Tom (1988). *Cardinal of the Kremlin, The*. G.P. Putnam & Son. ISBN 0-3991-3345-3.
- Clancy, Tom (1989). *Clear and Present Danger*. G.P. Putnam & Son. ISBN 0-3991-3440-9.
- Clancy, Tom (1991). *Sum of All Fears, The*. G.P. Putnam & Son. ISBN 0-3991-3615-0.
- Clancy, Tom (1993). *Without Remorse*. G.P. Putnam & Son. ISBN 0-3991-3825-0.
- Clancy, Tom (1994). *Debt of Honor*. G.P. Putnam & Son. ISBN 0-3991-3954-0.
- Clancy, Tom (1996). *Executive Orders*. G.P. Putnam & Son. ISBN 0-3991-4218-5.
- Clancy, Tom (1998). *Rainbow Six*. G.P. Putnam & Son. ISBN 0-3991-4390-4.
- Clancy, Tom (2000). *Bear and the Dragon, The*. G.P. Putnam & Son. ISBN 0-3991-4563-X.
- Clancy, Tom (2002). *Red Rabbit*. G.P. Putnam & Son. ISBN 0-3991-4870-1.
- Clancy, Tom (2003). *Teeth of the Tiger, The*. G.P. Putnam & Son. ISBN 0-3991-5079-X.

Patriot Games (film)

Patriot Games	
Theatrical poster	
Directed by	Phillip Noyce
Produced by	Mace Neufeld Robert G. Rehme
Written by	**Novel:** Tom Clancy **Screenplay:** W. Peter Iliff Donald E. Stewart Steven Zaillian
Starring	Harrison Ford Patrick Bergin Sean Bean Samuel L Jackson Anne Archer
Music by	James Horner
Cinematography	Donald M. McAlpine
Editing by	William Hoy Neil Travis
Distributed by	Paramount Pictures
Release date(s)	June 5, 1992
Running time	117 min.
Country	United States
Language	English
Budget	$25,300,200
Gross revenue	**Domestic:** $83,351,587 **Worldwide:** $178,051,587
Preceded by	*The Hunt for Red October (film)*
Followed by	*Clear and Present Danger*

Patriot Games is a 1992 film based on the novel of the same name by Tom Clancy, and is the sequel to the 1990 film the Hunt for Red October. It was released on June 5, 1992 and directed by Phillip Noyce. In the movie, Jack Ryan was played by Harrison Ford, Jack's surgeon-wife, Dr. Cathy Muller Ryan, by Anne Archer and the vengeful and psychopathic IRA terrorist, Sean Miller, is played by Sean Bean.

Plot

Jack Ryan (Ford) is on a "working vacation" in London with his family. He has retired from the CIA and is a Professor at the US Naval Academy. They witness a terrorist attack on Lord William Holmes, British Secretary of State for Northern Ireland and a distant member of the British Royal Family (the cousin of the Queen Mother). Ryan intervenes and kills one of the attackers, Patrick Miller, while his older brother Sean (Sean Bean) looks on. Ryan is badly wounded.

The remaining terrorists flee and leave Miller to be apprehended by the police. Whilst recovering, Ryan is called to testify in court against Sean Miller, who is part of the Ulster Liberation Army—a fictional breakaway group of the Provisional IRA. Ryan is awarded a knighthood—a KCVO: Knight Commander of the Victorian Order—and eventually returns to the United States.

While being transferred to Albany Prison on the Isle of Wight, Miller's escort convoy is ambushed by his ULA comrades who kill the police officers, and he escapes from custody. Miller and his companions flee Britain for North Africa to plan their next kidnapping attempt on Lord Holmes. Miller however, cannot shake his anger towards Ryan for killing his younger brother and persuades several members of his entourage to accompany him to the United States to murder Ryan and his family.

Ryan survives an attack outside the United States Naval Academy. Simultaneously, Miller and a colleague attack Ryan's wife and daughter as they're driving on a busy highway. They crash; both Cathy and her daughter are severely injured.

Enraged over the near-loss of his family, Ryan decides to go back to work for the CIA, having earlier rejected the appeal of his former superior, Vice Admiral James Greer (James Earl Jones).

Ryan's tireless work leads him to conclude that Miller has taken refuge in a training camp, one of many located in Libya. A SAS strike team attacks and kills everyone in the camp while Ryan looks on through a live satellite feed. But unbeknownst to Ryan, Miller and his companions had already fled the camp and were on their way to the US to stage their next attack on Lord Holmes.

Lord Holmes decides to visit Ryan at his home to formally present his KCVO. With the aid of Lord Holmes' traitorous assistant, Miller's group tracks Holmes to this location, kills the Diplomatic Security Service agents and Maryland state troopers guarding the house, and attempts once more to kidnap Lord Holmes. Ryan leads Holmes and his family to safety while he attempts to lure Miller and his companions away from his home.

The FBI Hostage Rescue Teams are scrambled to pick up Holmes. Upon realising that Ryan is leading them away from Holmes, Miller's companions try to persuade Miller to turn around, but an enraged and deranged Miller kills his terrorist companions and continues his pursuit of Ryan. Ryan and Miller fight hand to hand; Miller is killed when Ryan impales him backward on a boat anchor, and his body is obliterated in the subsequent explosion of the craft.

Credits roll just after Caroline Ryan learns the gender of the child she is going to have, and before she tells Jack and Sally.

Cast

- Harrison Ford as Jack Ryan
- Anne Archer as Dr. Caroline "Cathy" Ryan
- Patrick Bergin as Kevin O'Donnell
- Sean Bean as Sean Miller
- Thora Birch as Sally Ryan
- James Fox as Lord William Holmes
- Ellen Geer as Rose
- Samuel L. Jackson as Lieutenant Commander Robby Jackson
- Polly Walker as Annette
- J. E. Freeman as Marty Cantor
- James Earl Jones as Vice Admiral Jim Greer
- Richard Harris as Paddy O'Neil
- Alex Norton as Dennis Cooley
- Hugh Fraser as Geoffrey Watkins
- David Threlfall as Inspector Robert Highland

Production

Author Tom Clancy distanced himself from the movie because of a number of plot changes. Most significantly, the Prince became "Lord Holmes", the Queen Mother's cousin; and Sean Miller is killed at the end.

The movie was filmed in England and in the Washington, D.C. area including Annapolis, Maryland. However, skyscrapers shown in Annapolis are fictitious.

Harrison Ford accidentally hit Sean Bean with a boat hook while shooting the final scene; Bean has a scar over his eye as a result. (In Bean's subsequent *Sharpe* series, this would be emphasized with makeup to add credibility to his character.)

Casting

The actors who played Jack and Caroline Ryan in *The Hunt for Red October*, Alec Baldwin and Gates McFadden, were unavailable due to other commitments. At the time, Baldwin was performing *A Midsummer Night's Dream* on Broadway. McFadden, who appeared in "Red October" only for a moment, didn't accept "Patriot Games" greatly expanded screen role for Cathy Ryan due to her regular role as Dr. Beverly Crusher in *Star Trek: The Next Generation*. Despite the film's plot and setting, Richard Harris, Patrick Bergin and Jonathan Ryan, are the only Irish actors to appear in the film.

Music

The score by James Horner contains musical references to works by Aram Khachaturian (Adagio from "Gayane" Suite) and Dmitri Shostakovich *(Symphony No. 5, 3rd mvt.)*. One particular sequence in the music accompanying the scene in which Ryan, Greer, et al. view the live satellite feed of the SAS attack contains a nearly direct sampling from the latter.[*citation needed*] Horner's score is also very reminiscient in places of the score for Aliens (film).

A music video is shown in an early scene featuring Clannad's song "Theme from Harry's Game", originally made for an ITV drama about The Troubles in 1982. Patrick Bergin's character Kevin O'Donnell watches it during the scene where the Provisional IRA tries to kill him. Its appearance proved influential, and when the song was included on the *Patriot Games* soundtrack in 1992, it helped jump-start Clannad's popularity in the U.S.[*citation needed*]

When Jack Ryan meets Paddy O'Neil in the IRA bar the song "Pride of Our Land" can be heard in the background. The song is being performed by the band "Blended Spirits"

Differences between the book and film

There were several differences between the original novel and the film, some minor and some major. These include:

- In the book, Ryan visits London to carry out research in the WW2 naval archives. In the film, he is invited to give a talk to an audience of military officers.
- The entire storyline where Sean Miller wanted to attack Ryan because he killed his brother was not in the novel. His rage against Ryan was because he has never failed a mission before Ryan intervened, and he grew angrier when he failed to kill his wife and daughter.
- In the film Ryan saves Lord Holmes and his family; in the book he saves TRH The Prince and Princess of Wales and the newborn Prince William of Wales.
- In the book the Queen and the Prince of Wales visit Ryan while he is recovering in a London hospital; this doesn't happen in the film.
- Cathy tells Jack in the book while they are in England that she is pregnant. In the film Cathy tells Jack when they are back home

- In the film, when Sean Miller escaped, he executed the three police officers. In the novel, he spared their lives.
- In the film, a ULA operative was stalking Ryan as he exited the academy, they fought, and the soldier was soon killed by the gate guards. In the novel, Ryan was never hurt, the ULA operative was waiting outside the gates for Ryan to arrive, only for him to get unwanted attention by the gate guards and be promptly arrested.
- In the film, it was the British SAS that raided the camp in North Africa. In the novel, it was the French DGSE.
- In the film, Dennis Cooley, the rare-book collector and ULA informant, was executed by Sean Miller when he asked to come along on the operation. In the novel, Dennis actually was welcomed to join the raid.
- The climax where the ULA raid Ryan's home played out differently. In the novel, the ULA raided Ryan's home and managed to capture most of the inhabitants, until Robby Jackson managed to ambush them to get them outside. Everyone escaped down the cliff to the awaiting boats where a chase ensured, leading them all the way to the harbor of the Annapolis Academy, and they got many units to trap and corner Sean Miller and his small band on an ocean liner. Meanwhile, an FBI HRT unit arrived at the Ryan home to wipe out the surviving ULA members remaining. In the ocean liner, Ryan captures Sean Miller but doesn't kill him. Instead, he allows him to be captured by the police where he will get the death penalty for previously killing a police officer on US soil.
- At the very end of the movie, the viewer is left wondering what sex the child is (which was revealed in *Clear and Present Danger* that it was a boy). In the novel, Cathy gave birth to a son.

External links

- *Patriot Games (film)* [1] at the Internet Movie Database
- *Patriot Games* [2] at Allmovie
- *Patriot Games* [3] at Box Office Mojo

Clear and Present Danger (film)

Clear and Present Danger	
Theatrical release poster	
Directed by	Phillip Noyce
Written by	Novel: Tom Clancy **Screenplay:** Donald Stewart Steven Zaillian John Milius
Starring	Harrison Ford Willem Dafoe Anne Archer Miguel Sandoval Joaquim de Almeida James Earl Jones
Music by	James Horner
Editing by	Neil Travis
Distributed by	Paramount Pictures
Release date(s)	August 3, 1994
Running time	141 minutes
Country	United States
Language	English
Budget	$65,000,000
Gross revenue	$122,187,717 (Domestic) $215,887,717 (Worldwide)
Preceded by	*Patriot Games*
Followed by	*The Sum of All Fears*

Clear and Present Danger is a 1994 film directed by Phillip Noyce, based on the book of the same name by Tom Clancy. It is a sequel to the 1992 film *Patriot Games*.

It is the last film to feature Harrison Ford as Jack Ryan and James Earl Jones as Vice Admiral Greer, and the final one directed by Phillip Noyce.

As in the novel, Jack Ryan is appointed Central Intelligence Agency (CIA) Acting Deputy Director and discovers that he is being kept in the dark by colleagues who are conducting a covert war against drug lords in Colombia.

Plot

A United States Coast Guard patrol boat stops a suspicious yacht, finding an American businessman and his family have been murdered by several men operating the craft. The murdered man happens to have been a close friend of the President of the United States. President Bennett (Donald Moffat) learns that the man was murdered because of his ties to a drug cartel, having skimmed over $650 million from the cartel. The President tells James Cutter (Harris Yulin), his National Security Advisor, that Colombian drug cartels represent "a clear and present danger" to the U.S., indirectly giving Cutter unofficial permission to take down the men responsible for his friend's death.

Jack Ryan (Harrison Ford) is appointed Deputy Director (Intelligence) when his friend, mentor, and boss Admiral James Greer (James Earl Jones) is diagnosed with pancreatic cancer. Upon his appointment Ryan is asked to go before the United States Congress to request increased funding of $70 million for ongoing CIA intelligence operations in Colombia. Congress approves the funding, with Senator Mayo (Hope Lange) receiving Ryan's word that no troops or black-ops will be used.

Needing to keep an unwitting Ryan out of the loop, Cutter turns to CIA Deputy Director (Operations) Robert Ritter (Henry Czerny), who secures a document giving him permission to act as he sees fit to take down the cartel. Ritter assembles a black-ops team with the help of John Clark (Willem Dafoe), a secret field operative. Clark and his team travel to Colombia and begin destroying the various cartel gangs, their equipment and hidden drug lab facilities.

The head of one of the drug gangs, Ernesto Escobedo (Miguel Sandoval), is enraged at having lost over $600 million as a result of the freezing of assets, and has his intelligence officer, Félix Cortez (Joaquim de Almeida), take care of the problem. Cortez, a former colonel of Cuban military intelligence, has an unwitting contact inside the U.S. government — Moira Wolfson (Ann Magnuson), a secretary to Federal Bureau of Investigation (FBI) Director Emil Jacobs. Félix feigns romantic interest to discover that Jacobs is visiting Colombia to negotiate with the local attorney general concerning the frozen money.

Unaware of these covert dealings, Ryan finds himself caught in the middle of an assassination attempt on Jacobs, which only Ryan survives. Cortez travels to the U.S. and kills Moira to cover his tracks. Cortez's real motivation is to cause distrust among the leaders of the cartel (as none of them know who ordered the ambush of the FBI Director). Cortez believes he can assume control of the cartel following the gang war that will result.

In retaliation for the assassination of Jacobs, Cutter orders the bombing of a villa where the cartel's leaders are supposed to meet. The bombing is mostly successful, killing a large number of the cartel leaders and fooling the media and other observers into thinking that the destruction was caused by a car bomb set by a rival drug lord. Escobedo and Cortez avoid the bombing, but innocent women and children are killed in the action, much to Cutter's dismay. The situation is exacerbated when Ryan and Cortez independently discover that the United States was responsible for the bombing.

Cortez brokers a deal with Cutter. Cortez will assassinate Escobedo and take over the cartel, then reduce drug shipments to the U.S. and allow American law enforcement to arrest some of his workers at regular intervals so as to make the U.S. appear to be winning the drug war. In exchange, Cutter will shut down all operations in Colombia and allow Cortez to capture and kill Clark's soldiers. Cutter agrees and orders Ritter to get rid of all evidence of their operations and cut off the troops in Colombia from all support.

Ryan is told about the meeting between Cutter and Cortez. He hacks into Ritter's computer account and discovers Ritter's and Cutter's work in Colombia. Ritter notices Ryan's presence on the computer while he deletes all of the files, and the two men confront each other. Ritter tells Ryan that he has written permission from the President to do anything necessary to defeat the Cali Cartel, and so does Cutter. Jack will be the scapegoat for what has happened since he doesn't have that protection and was responsible for the funding from Congress that made the Colombian operations possible.

Greer succumbs to cancer. As the funeral takes place the black-ops team is ambushed in Colombia. Ryan goes to Colombia to find John Clark and save the soldiers. Ritter and Cutter find out about this and tell Clark that Ryan was responsible for the operations' shut-down. Clark almost kills Ryan before Ryan convinces him that Ritter and Cutter are responsible.

Clark hires a local retired American pilot and Ryan buys an aging Bell 412 helicopter. They fly to where the soldiers were attacked and find the squad's scout/sniper, Domingo Chavez (Raymond Cruz), who tells them that two of his unit members are imprisoned and the rest are dead. Ryan visits Escobedo's mansion and tell him what Cortez has been doing. Enraged, Escobedo accuses Cortez of treachery. One of Cortez's men kills Escobedo and henchmen, but is shot by Chávez. Ryan, Clark and Chávez rescue the prisoners, kill Cortez and escape.

Ryan confronts the President, who tries to convince Ryan that he now holds "a chip in the big game" — by being in the loop of what happened, Ryan can use the President for special favors; otherwise Ryan and Admiral Greer become the scapegoats. Ryan tells the President that he intends to blow the whistle at a Congressional Oversight Committee session despite the damage it could do to his career. He walks out of the Oval Office and begins his testimony to Congress.

Cast

- Harrison Ford as Jack Ryan
- Willem Dafoe as John Clark
- Anne Archer as Dr. Catherine "Cathy" Ryan
- Thora Birch as Sally Ryan
- Joaquim de Almeida as Col. Félix Cortez
- Henry Czerny as Robert Ritter, CIA Deputy Director for Operations
- Ellen Geer as Rose
- Harris Yulin as James Cutter, United States National Security Advisor
- Donald Moffat as President Bennett
- Miguel Sandoval as Ernesto Escobedo, leader of the Cali Cartel
- Benjamin Bratt as Captain Ramírez
- Raymond Cruz as Domingo Chávez
- James Earl Jones as Vice Admiral James Greer, CIA Deputy Director for Intelligence
- Dean Jones as Judge Moore
- Belita Moreno as Senior Special Agent Jean Fowler, DEA Task force Commander
- Tom Tammi as FBI Director Emile Jacobs
- Reg E. Cathey as Sergeant Major
- Jaime Gómez as Sgt. Julio Vega
- Greg Germann as Petey
- Ted Raimi as Satellite Analyst
- Rex Linn as Washington Detective
- Ann Magnuson as Moira Wolfson, Assistant to the Director of the FBI
- Hope Lange as Senator Mayo

Production notes

The final honors at Arlington National Cemetery are not in the correct order nor complete for what a U.S. Navy Admiral would receive. The portrayal was backwards and lacked the gun salute to which a flag officer is entitled.

External links

- *Clear and Present Danger* [1] at the Internet Movie Database
- *Clear and Present Danger* [2] at Box Office Mojo

Rick Deckard

Rick Deckard

Rick Deckard is the protagonist in Philip K. Dick's novel *Do Androids Dream of Electric Sheep?* as well as the 1982 film adaptation *Blade Runner* directed by Ridley Scott. In the film, Deckard is played by Harrison Ford.

Overview

In the film adaptation, Deckard is a "blade runner," a special member of the Los Angeles police department who is employed to hunt and "retire" artificial manufactured humanoids, called "replicants," as they have been declared illegal on Earth. At the beginning of the film, a group of unusually brutal replicants hijack a shuttle to Earth, intending to infiltrate their place of manufacture and extend their four-year lifespans. Deckard, formerly the best blade runner in the LAPD, is called out of retirement to hunt them down. He is reluctant to resume work, but its told he has no choice and must use some of "the old blade runner magic" to succeed. Deckard's character follows the model of a film noir detective, mixing old-fashioned sleuthing, interviewing suspects, and brutal violence. Like many noir heroes, he finds it hard to turn down a "damsel in distress," in this case the replicant Rachael, when she asks for his help. Despite being a skilled detective, Deckard is overmatched by the physically superior replicants, relying more on luck than actual fighting skill to defeat them.

In the novel, Deckard is an active bounty hunter working in San Francisco rather than retiring Los Angeles detective. He is tasked with hunting down six escaped replicants, called "androids" in the novel, who hope not to extend their lifespans, but simply to escape slavery on the colonies. The term "blade runner" is not used in the book.

Is Deckard a replicant?

There are lengthy debates among the movie's fandom on whether Deckard is a replicant himself. The Director's Cut DVD of the movie seems to lean towards the idea that Deckard is a replicant, as new footage was added that supports that side of the argument. In all versions of the film, Gaff's first line translates to "You are the blade, blade runner", and all versions of the film include Gaff leaving the unicorn origami figure in Deckard's apartment as a reference to Deckard's dream.

The purpose of this story as I saw it was that in his job of hunting and killing these replicants, Deckard becomes progressively dehumanized. At the same time, the replicants are being perceived as becoming more human. Finally,

Deckard must question what he is doing, and really what is the essential difference between him and them? And, to take it one step further, who is he if there is no real difference?

Philip K. Dick

The original novel includes a similar question, but in a more subtle form. It is made far more certain that Deckard is *not* an android. However, he *is* a Mercerist (he uses a device called an "empathy box" to commune with other humans in the experience of a mysterious, unknown man named Mercer, who may or may not exist; this is part of the evidence that he is not an android, as no android has ever been able to do this), and he makes use of a device called a "Penfield mood organ" which allows him to "dial" any emotion or state of mind he wishes to experience, at any moment, for reasons of practicality or pleasure. (Neither of these have any analogue in the film.) As such, although Deckard is physically human, the question of whether he is "human" by any meaning of the word in the reader's world is left open.

Actor Harrison Ford has stated that when he and director Ridley Scott were discussing the character prior to filming, they both agreed that Deckard was *not* a replicant. However, in multiple subsequent interviews, director Ridley Scott has come forward stating that Deckard *is* in fact a replicant. Ridley also states that Harrison Ford has given up the idea of Deckard being human.

In K.W. Jeter's Blade Runner novels, Rick Deckard is rediscovered by the Tyrell Corporation, who want to use him to retire the mysterious "sixth replicant" from the group he last hunted. (These novels use the character of Deckard as shown in the movie, not the original novel.) This mission ends up leading to further adventures involving various conspiracies between the Tyrell Corp., the United Nations, and Replicant Sympathizers.

See also

- Deckard: human or replicant?

External links

- The Blade Runner FAQ [1] – Is Deckard a Replicant?
- BBC: Blade Runner riddle solved [2] – Ridley Scott states his position.

Blade Runner

Blade Runner	
Original theatrical release poster	
Directed by	Ridley Scott
Produced by	Michael Deeley
Written by	Philip K. Dick
Screenplay by	• Hampton Fancher • David Peoples
Starring	• Harrison Ford • Rutger Hauer • Sean Young • Edward James Olmos
Music by	Vangelis
Cinematography	Jordan Cronenweth
Editing by	• Terry Rawlings • Marsha Nakashima • Les Healey (director's cut)
Studio	• The Ladd Company • Tandem Productions • Sir Run Run Shaw
Distributed by	Warner Bros. Pictures
Release date(s)	June 25, 1982
Running time	116 minutes (original theatrical cut) (See below for other versions)
Country	United States
Language	English
Budget	$28 million
Gross revenue	$32,768,670

Blade Runner is a 1982 American science fiction film, directed by Ridley Scott and starring Harrison Ford, Rutger Hauer, and Sean Young. The screenplay, written by Hampton Fancher and David Peoples, is based loosely on the novel *Do Androids Dream of Electric Sheep?* by Philip K. Dick.

The film depicts a dystopian Los Angeles in November 2019 in which genetically engineered organic robots called replicants—visually indistinguishable from adult humans—are manufactured by the all-powerful Tyrell Corporation as well as other mega manufacturers around the world. Their use on Earth is banned, and replicants are exclusively used for dangerous, menial or leisure work on Earth's off-world colonies. Replicants who defy the ban and return to Earth are hunted down and "retired" by police special operatives known as "blade runners". The plot focuses on a brutal and cunning group of recently escaped replicants hiding in Los Angeles and the burnt out expert blade runner, Rick Deckard, who reluctantly agrees to take on one more assignment to hunt them down.

Blade Runner initially polarized critics: some were displeased with the pacing, while others enjoyed its thematic complexity. The film performed poorly in North American theaters. Despite the box office failure of the film, it has since become a cult classic, and is now widely regarded as one of the best movies ever made. *Blade Runner* has been hailed for its production design, depicting a "retrofitted" future, and it remains a leading example of the neo-noir genre. *Blade Runner* brought the work of author Philip K. Dick to the attention of Hollywood, and several more films have since been based on his work. Ridley Scott regards *Blade Runner* as "probably" his most complete and personal film. In 1993, *Blade Runner* was selected for preservation in the United States National Film Registry by the Library of Congress as being "culturally, historically, or aesthetically significant".

Seven versions of the film have been shown for various markets as a result of controversial changes made by film executives. A rushed director's cut was released in 1992 after a strong response to workprint screenings. This, in conjunction with its popularity as a video rental, made it one of the first films released on DVD, resulting in a basic disc with mediocre video and audio quality. In 2007, Warner Bros. released in select theaters, and subsequently on DVD, HD DVD, and Blu-ray Disc, the 25th anniversary digitally remastered Final Cut by Scott.

Plot

In Los Angeles, November 2019, retired police officer Rick Deckard (Harrison Ford) is detained at a noodle bar by officer Gaff (Edward James Olmos). His former supervisor, Bryant (M. Emmet Walsh), tells him that several "replicants"—biologically engineered humanoids who serve as soldiers and slaves in off-world colonies—have escaped, and have come to Earth illegally. As a "blade runner" while active, Deckard's job was to track down replicants on Earth and "retire" them.

Bryant shows him a video of another blade runner, Holden (Morgan Paull), administering a Voight-Kampff test, which distinguishes humans from replicants based on their empathic response to questions. The subject of the test, Leon (Brion James), shoots Holden when it is likely he will be exposed as a replicant.

Deckard agrees to track down Leon and three other replicants—Roy Batty (Rutger Hauer), Zhora (Joanna Cassidy) and Pris (Daryl Hannah)—after Bryant threatens him. These replicants—Tyrell Corporation Nexus-6 models—have a four-year lifespan as a fail-safe to prevent them from developing emotions and desire for independence. They may have come to Earth to try to have these lifespans extended.

Deckard is teamed with Gaff and sent to the Tyrell Corporation to ensure that the Voight-Kampff test works on Nexus-6 models. While there, Deckard discovers that Tyrell's (Joe Turkel) assistant Rachael (Sean Young) is an experimental replicant who believes she is human; Rachael's consciousness has been enhanced with childhood memories from Tyrell's niece. As a result, a more extensive Voight-Kampff test is required to identify her as a replicant. During the testing Rachael suggests that Deckard himself be tested.

Roy and Leon enter the eye manufacturing laboratory of Chew (James Hong); under interrogation, Chew directs them to J.F. Sebastian (William Sanderson) as their best chance of meeting Tyrell. Rachael visits Deckard at his apartment to prove her humanity to him, showing him a family photo. She leaves in tears after Deckard tells her that her memories are implants. Pris meets J.F. Sebastian at his apartment in the Bradbury Building where he lives with his manufactured companions. Deckard finds an image of Zhora in Leon's photos.

Deckard goes to an area of the city where genetically engineered animals are sold to analyze a scale found in Leon's bathroom, learning that it came from a snake made by Abdul Ben Hassan (Ben Astar). Hassan directs Deckard to a strip club where Zhora works. Deckard "retires" Zhora, whose death takes place in slow motion as she struggles to flee. Deckard meets with Bryant shortly after and is told to add Rachael to his list of retirements, as she has disappeared from the Tyrell Corporation headquarters. Deckard spots Rachael in the crowd but is attacked by Leon. Rachael saves Deckard by killing Leon, and the two return to Deckard's apartment, where he prevents Rachael from leaving and gets her to say she wants to have sex with him.

Roy arrives at Sebastian's apartment and tells Pris they are the only ones left. They gain Sebastian's help after explaining their plight. Roy discovers that Sebastian is suffering from a genetic disorder that accelerates his aging. Under the pretext of Sebastian informing Tyrell of a winning move in a game of correspondence chess that they are playing, Roy and Sebastian enter Tyrell's penthouse. Roy demands an extension to his lifespan from his maker. Tyrell explains that Tyrell Corporation never found a way to accomplish this. Roy asks absolution for his sins, confessing that he has done "questionable things". Tyrell dismisses Roy's guilt, praising Roy's advanced design and his accomplishments. He tells Roy to "revel in his time", to which Roy comments "Nothing the god of biomechanics wouldn't let you into heaven for". Roy then holds Tyrell's head in his hands, gives him a kiss, and kills him. Sebastian runs for the elevator, with Roy following. Roy rides the elevator down alone, and Sebastian is not seen again.

Deckard arrives at Sebastian's apartment and is ambushed by Pris. He retires her just as Roy returns. Roy punches through a wall, grabbing Deckard's right arm, and breaks two of his fingers in retaliation for Zhora and Pris. Roy releases Deckard and gives him time to run before he begins hunting him through the Bradbury Building. The symptoms of Roy's limited lifespan worsen and his right hand begins failing; he jabs a nail through it to regain control. Roy forces Deckard to the roof. As Deckard attempts to escape Roy, he leaps across to another building but falls short and ends up hanging from a rain-slicked girder. As Deckard loses his grip, Roy, having made the same leap effortlessly, seizes his arm and hauls him onto the roof. As Roy's life ends, he delivers a soliloquy on his life "I've seen things you people wouldn't believe: Attack ships on fire off the shoulder of Orion; I've watched c-beams glitter in the dark near the Tannhauser Gate. All those moments will be lost in time; like tears in rain. Time to die."

Gaff arrives and shouts over to Deckard, "It's too bad she won't live; but then again, who does?" Deckard returns to his apartment to find Rachael alive. As they leave, Deckard finds an origami unicorn, a calling card left by Gaff. Depending on the version, the film ends with Deckard and Rachael either leaving the apartment block to an uncertain future or driving through an idyllic pastoral landscape.

Cast and characters

Main article: List of Blade Runner characters

With the exception of Harrison Ford, *Blade Runner* used a number of less well-known actors such as Daryl Hannah and Sean Young. The cast includes:

- Harrison Ford as Rick Deckard, coming off some success with *Star Wars* (1977), *The Empire Strikes Back* (1980) and *Raiders of the Lost Ark* (1981), Ford was looking for a role with dramatic depth. After Steven Spielberg praised Ford, he was hired for *Blade Runner*. In 1992, Ford revealed, "*Blade Runner* is not one of my favorite films. I tangled with Ridley." Apart from friction with the director, Ford also disliked the voiceovers: "When we started shooting it had been tacitly agreed that the version of the film that we had agreed upon was the version without voiceover narration. It was a f**king [*sic*] nightmare. I thought that the film had worked without the narration. But now I was stuck re-creating that narration. And I was obliged to do the voiceovers for people that did not represent the director's interests." "I went kicking and screaming to the studio to record it."
- Rutger Hauer as Roy Batty, the violent yet thoughtful leader of replicants; regarded by Philip K. Dick as "the perfect Batty—cold, Aryan, flawless". Of the many films Hauer has done, *Blade Runner* is his favorite. As he explained in a live chat in 2001, "BLADE RUNNER needs no explanation. It just IZZ [*sic*]. All of the best. There is nothing like it. To be part of a real MASTERPIECE which changed the world's thinking. It's awesome."
- Sean Young as Rachael, Tyrell's assistant. Rachael is a replicant with memories that belonged to Tyrell's niece.
- Edward James Olmos as Gaff, Olmos used his diverse ethnic background, and some in-depth personal research, to help create the fictional "Cityspeak" language his character uses in the film. His initial addresses to Deckard at the noodle bar is partly in Hungarian, and means, "Horse dick!

No way. You are the Blade ... Blade Runner."

- Daryl Hannah as Pris, a "basic pleasure model". The development of her relationship with Roy Batty is shown as a symbol of the replicants' underlying humanity.
- M. Emmet Walsh as Captain Bryant, Walsh lived up to his reputation as a great character actor with the role of a hard-drinking, sleazy and underhanded police veteran typical of the film noir genre.
- Joe Turkel as Dr. Eldon Tyrell, a corporate mogul who has built an empire on genetically manipulated humanoid slaves.
- William Sanderson as J. F. Sebastian, a quiet and lonely genius who provides a compassionate yet compliant portrait of humanity. J.F. is able to sympathize with the replicants' short lifespan because he has "Methuselah Syndrome" (possibly a form of progeria), a genetic disease that causes faster aging and a short lifespan.
- Brion James as Leon Kowalski, a replicant masquerading as a waste disposal engineer; he shoots a Blade Runner to escape, establishing the physical threat the replicants pose to their would-be captors.
- Joanna Cassidy as Zhora, a special-ops, undercover and assassin model. Cassidy portrays a strong female replicant who has seen the worst humanity has to offer.
- Morgan Paull as Holden, the Blade Runner initially assigned to the case, he is shot by Leon while screening new Tyrell employees in an attempt to find the replicants, prompting his replacement with Deckard.
- James Hong as Hannibal Chew, an elderly Asian geneticist specializing in synthetic eyes.
- Hy Pyke as Taffey Lewis, Pyke conveys Lewis's sleaziness with ease and with one take; something almost unheard-of with Scott's drive for perfection resulting at times in double-digit takes.

Production

One of filming locations is Bradbury Building in Los Angeles.

Interest in adapting Philip K. Dick's novel *Do Androids Dream of Electric Sheep?* developed shortly after its 1968 publication. According to Dick, director Martin Scorsese was interested in filming the novel, but never optioned it. Producer Herb Jaffe optioned it in the early 1970s, but Dick wasn't impressed with the screenplay: "Robert Jaffe, who wrote the screenplay, flew down here to Orange County. I said to him then that it was so bad that I wanted to know if he wanted me to beat him up there at the airport or wait till we got to my apartment." The screenplay by Hampton Fancher was optioned in 1977.

Producer Michael Deeley became interested in Fancher's draft and convinced director Ridley Scott to use it to create his first American film. Scott had previously declined the project, but after leaving the slow production of *Dune*, wanted a faster-paced project to take his mind off his older brother's recent death. He joined the project on February 21, 1980, and managed to push up the promised financing from Filmways from $13 million to $15 million. Fancher's script focused more on environmental issues and less on issues of humanity and faith, which weighed heavily in the novel. Scott wanted changes. Fancher found a cinema treatment by William S. Burroughs for Alan E. Nourse's novel *The Bladerunner* (1974), entitled *Blade Runner (a movie)*. Scott liked the name, so Deeley obtained the rights to the titles. Eventually he hired David Peoples to rewrite the script, and Fancher left the job on December 21, 1980, over the issue, although he later returned to contribute additional rewrites.

Having invested over $2.5 million in pre-production, as the date of commencement of principal photography neared, Filmways withdrew financial backing. In ten days, Deeley secured $21.5 million in financing through a three way deal between The Ladd Company (through Warner Bros.), the Hong Kong-based producer Sir Run Run Shaw, and Tandem Productions.

Philip K. Dick became concerned that no one had informed him about the film's production, which added to his distrust of Hollywood. After Dick criticized an early version of Hampton Fancher's script in an article written for the Los Angeles *Select TV Guide*, the studio sent Dick the David Peoples rewrite. Although Dick died shortly before the film's release, he was pleased with the rewritten script, and with a twenty-minute special effects test reel that was screened for him when he was invited to the studio. Dick enthused after the screening to Ridley Scott that the world created for the film looked exactly as he had imagined it. The motion picture was dedicated to Dick.

Another shot of Bradbury Building.

Blade Runner has numerous and deep similarities to Fritz Lang's *Metropolis*, including a built up urban environment, in which the wealthy literally live above the workers, dominated by a huge building—the Stadtkrone Tower in *Metropolis* and the Tyrell Building in *Blade Runner*. Special effects supervisor David Dryer used stills from *Metropolis* when lining up *Blade Runner*'s miniature building shots.

Ridley Scott credits Edward Hopper's painting *Nighthawks* and the French science fiction comic magazine *Métal Hurlant* (Heavy Metal), to which the artist Moebius contributed, as stylistic mood sources. He also drew on the landscape of "Hong Kong on a very bad day" and the industrial landscape of his one-time home in the North East of England. Scott hired as his conceptual artist Syd Mead, who, like Scott, was influenced by *Métal Hurlant*. Moebius was offered the opportunity to assist in the pre-production of *Blade Runner*, but he declined so that he could work on René Laloux's animated film *Les Maîtres du temps*, a decision he later regretted. Lawrence G. Paull (production designer) and David Snyder (art director) realized Scott's and Mead's sketches. Douglas

Trumbull and Richard Yuricich supervised the special effects for the film. Principal photography of *Blade Runner* began on March 9, 1981, and ended four months later.

Casting the film proved troublesome, particularly for the lead role of Deckard. Screenwriter Hampton Fancher envisioned Robert Mitchum as Deckard, and wrote the character's dialogue with Mitchum in mind. Director Ridley Scott and the film's producers "spent months" meeting and discussing the role with Dustin Hoffman, who eventually departed over differences in vision. Harrison Ford was ultimately chosen for several reasons, including his performance in the *Star Wars* films, Ford's interest in the story of *Blade Runner*, and discussions with Steven Spielberg, who was finishing *Raiders of the Lost Ark* at the time and strongly praised Ford's work in the film. According to production documents, a long list of actors were considered for the role, including, but not limited to, Gene Hackman, Sean Connery, Jack Nicholson, Paul Newman, Clint Eastwood, Tommy Lee Jones, Arnold Schwarzenegger, Al Pacino, and Burt Reynolds.

Casting the roles of Rachael and Pris was also challenging; a lengthy series of screen tests were filmed with numerous actresses auditioning for the roles. Morgan Paull, who played the role of Deckard during the screen tests with actresses auditioning for the role of Rachael and Pris, was cast as Deckard's fellow bounty hunter Holden based on his performances in the tests. Among the actresses tested for the role of Rachael was blonde Nina Axelrod, who was Paull's recommendation. Stacey Nelkin tried out for Pris, but was instead given another role in the film, which was ultimately cut before filming. Both Axelrod's and Nelkin's screen tests are featured in the 2007 documentary *Dangerous Days: Making Blade Runner*.

One role that was not difficult to cast was Roy Batty: Ridley Scott cast Rutger Hauer without having met him, based solely on Hauer's performances in other films Scott had seen. Joe Pantoliano, who later played the role of Cypher in *The Matrix*, was considered for the role of Sebastian.

In 2006, Ridley Scott was asked "Who's the biggest pain in the arse you've ever worked with?" He replied: "It's got to be Harrison ... he'll forgive me because now I get on with him. Now he's become charming. But he knows a lot, that's the problem. When we worked together it was my first film up and I was the new kid on the block. But we made a good movie." Ford said of Scott in 2000: "I admire his work. We had a bad patch there, and I'm over it." More recently in 2006, Ford reflected on the production of the film saying: "What I remember more than anything else when I see *Blade Runner* is not the 50 nights of shooting in the rain, but the voiceover ... I was still obliged to work for these clowns that came in writing one bad voiceover after another." Ridley Scott confirmed in the summer 2007 issue of *Total Film* that Harrison Ford contributed to the *Blade Runner* Special Edition DVD, having already done his interviews. "Harrison's fully on board", said Scott.

Interpretation

Main article: Themes in Blade Runner

Although *Blade Runner* is ostensibly an action film, it operates on multiple dramatic and narrative levels; it is greatly indebted to film noir conventions: the femme fatale, protagonist-narration (removed in later versions), dark and shadowy cinematography, and the questionable moral outlook of the hero—in this case, extended to include reflections upon the nature of his own humanity.

It is a literate science fiction film, thematically enfolding the philosophy of religion and moral implications of human mastery of genetic engineering in the context of classical Greek drama and hubris, and draws on Biblical images, such as Noah's flood, and literary sources, such as *Frankenstein*. Linguistically, the theme of mortality is subtly reiterated in the chess game between Roy and Tyrell based on the famous Immortal game of 1851, though Scott has said that was coincidental.

Blade Runner delves into the implications of technology for the environment and society by reaching to the past, using literature, religious symbolism, classical dramatic themes, and film noir. This tension, between past, present, and future is mirrored in the retrofitted future of Blade Runner, which is high-tech and gleaming in places but decayed and old elsewhere. Interviewing Ridley Scott in 2002, reporter Lynn Barber in *The Observer* described the film as: "extremely dark, both literally and metaphorically, with an oddly masochistic feel". Director Scott said he "liked the idea of exploring pain" in the wake of his brother's skin cancer death. "When he was ill, I used to go and visit him in London, and that was really traumatic for me."

An aura of paranoia suffuses the film. Corporate power looms large, the police seem omnipresent, vehicle and warning lights probe into buildings, and the consequences of huge biomedical power over the individual are explored—especially the consequences for replicants of their programming. Control over the environment is depicted as taking place on a vast scale, hand in hand with the absence of any natural life, with artificial animals substituting for their extinct templates. This oppressive backdrop explains the frequently referenced migration of humans to extra-terrestrial ("off-world") colonies. The dystopian themes explored in "Blade Runner" are an early example of cyberpunk concepts expanding into film. Eyes are a recurring motif, as are manipulated images, calling into question reality and our ability to accurately perceive and remember it.

These thematic elements provide an atmosphere of uncertainty for *Blade Runner's* central theme of examining humanity. In order to discover replicants, an empathy test is used, with a number of its questions focused on the treatment of animals—it seems to be an essential indicator of someone's "humanity". The replicants are juxtaposed with human characters who lack empathy, while the replicants appear to show compassion and concern for one another at the same time as the mass of humanity on the streets is cold and impersonal. The film goes so far as to put in doubt whether Deckard is a human, and forces the audience to reevaluate what it means to be human.

The question of whether Deckard is intended to be a human or a replicant has been an ongoing controversy since the film's release. Both Michael Deeley and Harrison Ford wanted Deckard to be human while Hampton Fancher preferred ambiguity. Ridley Scott has confirmed that in his vision Deckard is a replicant. Deckard's unicorn dream sequence inserted into the Director's Cut coinciding with Gaff's parting-gift of an origami unicorn is seen by many as showing Deckard is a replicant as Gaff could have access to Deckard's implanted memories. The interpretation that Deckard is a replicant is challenged by others who believe unicorn imagery shows that the characters, whether human or replicant, share the same dreams and recognise their affinity, or that the absence of a decisive answer is crucial to the film's main theme. The inherent ambiguity and uncertainty of the film, as well as its textual richness, have permitted viewers to see it from their own perspectives.

The novel and the film

As a result of Fancher's divergence from the novel, numerous re-writes before and throughout shooting the film, and Ridley Scott's never having read the entire novel on which it was based, the film differed significantly from its original inspiration.

Some of the themes in the novel that were minimized or entirely removed include: fertility/sterility of the population; religion; mass media; Deckard's marriage; duality of Rachel and Pris; curiosity/fear of the psychological implications of sex with androids; Deckard's uncertainty that he is human; and real versus synthetic pets and emotions.

Philip K. Dick refused an offer of $400,000 to write a novelization of the *Blade Runner* screenplay, saying: "[I was] told the cheapo novelization would have to appeal to the twelve-year-old audience" and "[it] would have probably been disastrous to me artistically." He added, "That insistence on my part of bringing out the original novel and not doing the novelization—they were just furious. They finally recognized that there was a legitimate reason for reissuing the novel, even though it cost them money. It was a victory not just of contractual obligations but of theoretical principles." In the end, *Do Androids Dream of Electric Sheep?* was reprinted as a tie-in, with the film poster as a cover and the original title in parentheses below the *Blade Runner* title.

The producers of the film arranged for a screening of some special effects rough cuts for Philip K. Dick shortly before he died in early 1982. Despite his well known skepticism of Hollywood in principle, he became quite enthusiastic about the film. He said, "I saw a segment of Douglas Trumbull's special effects for *Blade Runner* on the KNBC-TV news. I recognized it immediately. It was my own interior world. They caught it perfectly." He also approved of the film's script, saying, "After I finished reading the screenplay, I got the novel out and looked through it. The two reinforce each other, so that someone who started with the novel would enjoy the movie and someone who started with the movie would enjoy the novel."

Reception

Blade Runner was released in 1,290 theaters on June 25, 1982. That date was chosen by producer Alan Ladd, Jr. because his previous highest-grossing films (*Star Wars* and *Alien*) had a similar opening date (May 25) in 1977 and 1979, making the date his "lucky day". However, the gross for the opening weekend was a disappointing $6.15 million. A significant factor in the film's rather poor box office performance was that its release coincided with other science fiction film releases, including *The Thing*, *Star Trek II: The Wrath of Khan*, and, most significantly, *E.T. the Extra-Terrestrial*, which dominated box office revenues that summer.

Film critics were polarized as some felt the story had taken a back seat to special effects and that it was not the action/adventure the studio had advertised. Others acclaimed its complexity and predicted it would stand the test of time.

In the United States, a general criticism was its slow pacing that detracts from other strengths; Sheila Benson from the *Los Angeles Times* called it "Blade crawler", while Pat Berman in State and Columbia Record described it as "science fiction pornography". Roger Ebert praised both the original and the *Director's cut* version of *Blade Runner*'s visuals and recommended it for that reason; however, he found the human story clichéd and a little thin. In 2007, upon release of *The Final Cut*, Roger Ebert somewhat revised his original opinion of the film and added it to his list of Great Movies, saying "I have been assured that my problems in the past with "Blade Runner" represent a failure of my own taste and imagination, but if the film was perfect, why has Sir Ridley continued to tinker with it?"

Accolades

Blade Runner has won and been nominated for the following awards:

Year	Award	Category	Nominee	Result
1982	British Society of Cinematographers	Best Cinematography Award	Jordan Cronenweth	Nominated
1982	Los Angeles Film Critics Association Award	Best Cinematography	Jordan Cronenweth	Won

1983	BAFTA Film Award	Best Cinematography	Jordan Cronenweth	Won
		Best Costume Design	Charles Knode & Michael Kaplan	Won
		Best Production Design/Art Direction	Lawrence G. Paull	Won
		Best Film Editing	Terry Rawlings	Nominated
		Best Make Up Artist	Marvin Westmore	Nominated
		Best Score	Vangelis	Nominated
		Best Sound	Peter Pennell, Bud Alper, Graham V. Hartstone, Gerry Humphreys	Nominated
		Best Special Visual Effects	Douglas Trumbull, Richard Yuricich, David Dryer	Nominated
1983	Hugo Award	Best Dramatic Presentation	*Blade Runner*	Won
1983	London Critics Circle Film Awards	Special Achievement Award	Lawrence G. Paull, Douglas Trumbull, Syd Mead	Won
1983	Golden Globes	Best Original Score - Motion Picture	Vangelis	Nominated
1983	Academy Awards	Best Art Direction - Set Decoration	Lawrence G. Paull, David L. Snyder, Linda DeScenna	Nominated
		Best Effects, Visual Effects	Douglas Trumbull, Richard Yuricich, David Dryer	Nominated
1983	Saturn Award	Best Science Fiction Film	*Blade Runner*	Nominated
		Best Director	Ridley Scott	Nominated
		Best Special Effects	Douglas Trumbull, Richard Yuricich	Nominated
		Best Supporting Actor	Rutger Hauer	Nominated
1983	Fantasporto	International Fantasy Film Award	Best Film – Ridley Scott	Nominated
1993	Fantasporto	International Fantasy Film Award	Best Film – Ridley Scott (Director's cut)	Nominated
1994	Saturn Award	Best Genre Video Release	*Blade Runner* (Director's cut)	Nominated
2008	Saturn Award	Best DVD Special Edition Release	*Blade Runner* (5 Disc Ultimate Collector's Edition)	Won

Lists of the best films

Current recognitions for *Blade Runner* include:

- Blade Runner is currently ranked the third best film of all time by The Screen Directory.
- British movie magazine *Empire* voted it the "Best Science Fiction Film Ever" in 2007.
- In 2002, *Blade Runner* was voted the 8th greatest film of all time in Channel 4's 100 Greatest Films poll.
- *New Scientist* readers voted it as the "all-time favourite science fiction" film in October 2008.

<table>
<tr><th>Year</th><th>Presenter</th><th>Title</th><th>Rank</th><th>Notes</th></tr>
<tr><td rowspan="2">2008</td><td>Empire</td><td>The 500 Greatest Movies of All Time</td><td>20</td><td></td></tr>
<tr><td rowspan="2">American Film Institute (AFI)</td><td>Top 10 Sci-fi Films of All Time</td><td>6</td><td></td></tr>
<tr><td>2007</td><td>AFI's 100 Years...100 Movies</td><td>97</td><td></td></tr>
<tr><td>2006</td><td>Total Film's Readers</td><td rowspan="2">100 Greatest Movies of All Time</td><td>32</td><td></td></tr>
<tr><td rowspan="2">2005</td><td>Total Film's Editors</td><td>47</td><td></td></tr>
<tr><td>Time Magazine's Critics</td><td>"All-TIME" 100 Best Movies</td><td>None</td><td></td></tr>
<tr><td>2004</td><td>The Guardian, Scientists</td><td>Top 10 Sci-fi Films of All Time</td><td>1</td><td></td></tr>
<tr><td>2003</td><td colspan="2">1001 Movies You Must See Before You Die</td><td rowspan="2">None</td><td></td></tr>
<tr><td rowspan="2">2002</td><td colspan="2">50 Klassiker, Film</td><td></td></tr>
<tr><td>Online Film Critics Society (OFCS)</td><td>Top 100 Sci-fi Films of the Past 100 Years</td><td>2</td><td></td></tr>
</table>

Cultural influence

While not initially a success with North American audiences, the film was popular internationally and became a cult film. The film's dark style and futuristic design have served as a benchmark and its influence can be seen in many subsequent science fiction films, anime, video games, and television programs. For example, Ronald D. Moore and David Eick, the producers of the re-imagining of *Battlestar Galactica*, have both cited *Blade Runner* as one of the major influences for the show. *Blade Runner* continues to reflect modern trends and concerns, and an increasing number consider it one of the greatest science fiction films of all time. The film was selected for preservation in the United States National Film Registry in 1993 and is frequently used in university courses. In 2007, it was named the 2nd most visually influential film of all time by the Visual Effects Society.

Blade Runner is one of the most musically sampled films of the 20th century, and inspired the Grammy nominated song "More Human than Human" by White Zombie. The 2009 album, *I, Human*, by Singaporean band Deus Ex Machina makes numerous references to the genetic engineering and cloning themes from the film, and even feature a track entitled "Replicant".

Blade Runner has influenced adventure games, such as *Rise of the Dragon*, *Snatcher*, *Beneath a Steel Sky* and *Flashback: The Quest for Identity*, the anime series *Bubblegum Crisis*, the role-playing game *Shadowrun*, the first-person shooter *Perfect Dark*, and the *Syndicate* series of video games.[*citation needed*] The film is also cited as the a major influence on Warren Spector, designer of the computer-game *Deus Ex*, which both in its visual rendering and plot displays evidence of the film's influence. The look of the film (darkness, neon lights and opacity of vision) is easier to render than complicated backdrops, making it a popular choice for game designers.

Blade Runner has also been the subject of parody, such as the comics *Blade Bummer* by *Crazy* comics, *Bad Rubber* by Steve Gallacci, and the *Red Dwarf* special episodes, "Back To Earth".

Blade Runner curse

Among the folklore that has developed around the film over the years has been the belief that the film was a curse to the companies whose logos were displayed prominently as product placements in some scenes. While they were market leaders at the time, more than half experienced disastrous setbacks during the next decade. RCA, which at one time was the United States' leading consumer electronics and communications conglomerate, was bought out by one-time parent General Electric in 1985, and dismantled. Atari, which dominated the home video game market when the film came out, never recovered from the next year's downturn in the industry, and by the 1990s had ceased to represent anything more than a brand, a back catalogue of games and some legacy computers. Atari today is an entirely different firm, using the former company's name. Cuisinart similarly went bankrupt in 1989, though it lives on under new ownership. The Bell System monopoly was broken up that same year, and most of the resulting Regional Bell operating companies have since changed their names and merged back with each other and other companies to form the new AT&T. Pan Am suffered from the terrorist bombing/destruction of Pan Am Flight 103 and after a decade of mounting losses, finally went bankrupt in 1991 with the falloff in overseas travel caused by the Gulf War. The Coca-Cola Company suffered losses during its failed introduction of New Coke in 1985, but soon afterward regained its market share. Its continued success has made Coca-Cola one of several exceptions to the *Blade Runner* curse; also appearing in the film are logos for Budweiser, and the electronics company TDK, which continue to thrive in contemporary markets.

Future Noir

Further information: Tech noir

Before the film's principal photography began, *Cinefantastique* magazine commissioned Paul M. Sammon to write an article about *Blade Runner*'s production, which became the book *Future Noir: The Making of Blade Runner* (referred to as the "*Blade Runner* Bible" by many of the film's fans). The book chronicles the evolution of *Blade Runner* as a film, and focuses on film-set politics, especially the British director's experiences with his first American film crew, of which producer Alan Ladd, Jr. has said, "Harrison wouldn't speak to Ridley and Ridley wouldn't speak to Harrison. By the end of the shoot Ford was 'ready to kill Ridley', said one colleague. He really would have taken him on if he hadn't been talked out of it." *Future Noir* has short cast biographies and quotations about their experiences in making *Blade Runner*, as well as many photographs of the film's production, and preliminary sketches. The cast chapter was deleted from the first edition; it is available online. A second edition of *Future Noir* was published in 2007.

Soundtrack

Main article: Blade Runner (soundtrack)

The *Blade Runner* soundtrack by Vangelis is a dark melodic combination of classic composition and futuristic synthesizers which mirrors the film-noir retro-future envisioned by Ridley Scott. Vangelis, fresh from his Academy Award winning score for *Chariots of Fire*, composed and performed the music on his synthesizers. He also made use of various chimes and the vocals of collaborator Demis Roussos. Another memorable sound is the haunting tenor sax solo "Love Theme" by UK saxophonist Dick Morrissey, who appeared on many of Vangelis' albums. Ridley Scott also used "Memories of Green" from Vangelis' album *See You Later* (an orchestral version of which Scott would later use in his film *Someone To Watch Over Me*).

Along with Vangelis' compositions and ambient textures, the film's sound scape also features a track by the Japanese Ensemble Nipponia ('Ogi No Mato' or 'The Folding Fan as a Target' from the Nonesuch Records release "Traditional Vocal And Instrumental Music") and a track by harpist Gail Laughton ("Harps of the Ancient Temples" from Laurel Records).

Despite being well received by fans and critically acclaimed and nominated in 1983 for a BAFTA and Golden Globe as best original score, and the promise of a soundtrack album from Polydor Records in the end titles of the film, the release of the official soundtrack recording was delayed for over a decade. There are two official releases of the music from *Blade Runner*. In light of the lack of a release of an album, the New American Orchestra recorded an orchestral adaptation in 1982 which bore little resemblance to the original. Some of the film tracks would in 1989 surface on the compilation *Vangelis: Themes*, but not until the 1992 release of the Director's Cut version would a substantial amount of the film's score see commercial release.

These delays and poor reproductions led to the production of many bootleg recordings over the years. A bootleg tape surfaced in 1982 at science fiction conventions and became popular given the delay of an official release of the original recordings, and in 1993 "Off World Music, Ltd." created a bootleg CD that would prove more comprehensive than Vangelis' official CD in 1994. A disc from "Gongo Records" features most of the same material, but with slightly better sound quality. In 2003, two other bootlegs surfaced, the "Esper Edition", closely preceded by "Los Angeles: November 2019". The double disc "Esper Edition" combined tracks from the official release, the Gongo boot and the film itself. Finally "2019" provided a single disc compilation almost wholly consisting of ambient sound from the film, padded out with some sounds from the Westwood game *Blade Runner*.

A set with three CDs of *Blade Runner*-related Vangelis music was released on December 10, 2007. Titled *Blade Runner Trilogy*, the first CD contains the same tracks as the 1994 official soundtrack release, the second CD contains previously unreleased music from the movie, and the third CD is all newly composed music from Vangelis, inspired by, and in the spirit of the movie.

Versions

Main article: Versions of Blade Runner

Seven different versions of *Blade Runner* have been shown:

- Original **workprint version** (1982, 113 minutes) shown to audience test previews in Denver and Dallas in March 1982. It was also seen in 1990 and 1991 in Los Angeles and San Francisco as a *Director's Cut* without Scott's approval. Negative responses to the test previews led to the modifications resulting in the U.S. theatrical version, while positive response to the showings in 1990 and 1991 pushed the studio to approve work on an official director's cut. It was re-released with 5-disc Ultimate Edition in 2007.
- A **San Diego Sneak Preview** shown only once in May 1982, which was almost identical to the *Domestic Cut* with three extra scenes.
- The **U.S. theatrical version** (1982, 116 minutes), known as the original version or *Domestic Cut*, released on Betamax and VHS in 1983 and laserdisc in 1987.
- The **International Cut** (1982, 117 minutes) also known as the "Criterion Edition" or uncut version, included more violent action scenes than the U.S. theatrical version. Although initially unavailable in the U.S. and distributed in Europe and Asia via theatrical and local Warner Home Video laserdisc releases, it was later released on VHS and Criterion Collection laserdisc in North America, and re-released in 1992 as a "10th Anniversary Edition".
- The **U.S. broadcast version** (1986, 114 minutes), the U.S. theatrical version edited for violence, profanity and nudity by CBS to meet broadcast restrictions.
- The Ridley Scott-approved (1992, 116 minutes) **Director's Cut**; prompted by the unauthorized 1990 – 1 workprint theatrical release and made available on VHS and laserdisc in 1993, and on DVD in 1997. Significant changes from the theatrical version include removal of Deckard's voice-over, re-insertion of a unicorn sequence and removal of the studio-imposed happy ending. Ridley did provide extensive notes and consultation to Warner Bros. through film preservationist Michael Arick who was put in charge of creating the Director's Cut.
- Ridley Scott's **Final Cut** (2007, 117 minutes), or the "25th Anniversary Edition", released by Warner Bros. theatrically on October 5, 2007, and subsequently released on DVD, HD DVD, and Blu-ray in December 2007 (U.K. December 3; U.S. December 18). This is the only version over which Ridley Scott had complete artistic control as he was not directly in charge of the *Director's*

Cut. In conjunction with the *Final Cut*, extensive documentary and other materials were produced for the home video releases culminating in a five-disc "Ultimate Collector's Edition" release by Charles de Lauzirika.

Derivative works

Documentaries

On the Edge of Blade Runner (2000)

On the Edge of Blade Runner (55 minutes) was produced in 2000 by Nobles Gate Ltd. (for Channel 4), was directed by Andrew Abbott and hosted/written by Mark Kermode. Interviews with production staff, including Scott, give details of the creative process and the turmoil during preproduction. Stories from Paul M. Sammon and Hampton Fancher provide insight into Philip K. Dick and the origins of *Do Androids Dream of Electric Sheep?*

Interwoven are cast interviews (with the notable exceptions of Harrison Ford and Sean Young), which convey some of the difficulties of making the film (including an exacting director and humid, smoggy weather). There is also a tour of some locations, most notably the Bradbury Building and the Warner Bros. backlot that became the LA 2019 streets, which look very different from Scott's dark vision.

The documentary then details the test screenings and the resulting changes (the voice over, the happy ending, and the deleted Holden hospital scene), the special effects, the soundtrack by Vangelis, and the unhappy relationship between the filmmakers and the investors which culminated in Deeley and Scott being fired but still working on the film. The question of whether or not Deckard is a replicant surfaces.

Future Shocks (2003)

Future Shocks (27 minutes) is a more recent documentary from 2003 by TVOntario (part of their *Film 101* series using footage compiled over the years for Saturday Night at the Movies). It includes interviews with executive producer Bud Yorkin, Syd Mead, and the cast, this time with Sean Young, but still without Harrison Ford. There is extensive commentary by science fiction author Robert J. Sawyer and from film critics, as the documentary focuses on the themes, visual impact and influence of the film. Edward James Olmos describes Ford's participation, and personal experiences during filming are related by Young, Walsh, Cassidy and Sanderson. They also relate a story about crew members creating T-shirts that took pot shots at Scott. The different versions of the film are critiqued and the accuracy of its predictions of the future are discussed.

Dangerous Days (2007)

Dangerous Days: Making Blade Runner is an approximately three and a half hour long documentary directed and produced by Charles de Lauzirika for the 2007 Final Cut version of the film. It appears with every edition of *The Final Cut* on DVD, HD DVD and Blu-ray. (It is a DVD format disc, even in the HD DVD and Blu-ray editions). It was culled from over 80 interviews, including Harrison Ford, Sean Young, Rutger Hauer, Edward James Olmos, Jerry Perenchio, Bud Yorkin and Ridley Scott, and also contains several alternate and deleted shots within the context of the documentary itself.

The documentary consists of eight chapters, each covering a portion of the film-making—or in the case of the final chapter, the film's controversial legacy. The chapters and their length:

- Incept Date – 1980: Screenwriting and Dealmaking – 30:36
- Blush Response: Assembling the Cast – 22:46
- A Good Start: Designing the Future – 26:34
- Eye of the Storm: Production Begins – 28:48
- Living in Fear: Tension on the Set – 29:23
- Beyond the Window: Visual effects – 28:49
- In Need of Magic: Post-Production Problems – 23:05
- To Hades and Back: Release and Resurrection – 24:12

All Our Variant Futures (2007)

All Our Variant Futures: From Workprint to Final Cut (29 minutes), produced by Paul Prischman, appears on Disc 5 of the *Blade Runner* Ultimate Collector's Edition and provides an overview of the film's multiple versions and their origins, as well as detailing the seven year-long restoration, enhancement and remastering process behind *The Final Cut.* Included are interviews with director Ridley Scott, restoration producer Charles de Lauzirika, restoration consultant Kurt P. Galvao, restoration VFX supervisor John Scheele and *Future Noir: The Making of Blade Runner* author Paul M. Sammon. Behind-the-scenes footage documenting the restoration—from archival work done in 2001 through the 2007 filming of Joanna Cassidy and Benjamin Ford for *The Final Cut*'s digital fixes—are seen throughout.

Additional featurettes (2007)

In addition to *Dangerous Days: Making Blade Runner*, a variety of other supplemental featurettes produced and directed by Charles de Lauzirika are included both the four- and five-disc collector's editions of *Blade Runner* released by Warner Home Video in 2007:

- The Electric Dreamer: Remembering Philip K. Dick – 14:22
- Sacrificial Sheep: The Novel Vs. The Film – 15:07
- Philip K. Dick: The *Blade Runner* Interviews – 23:03
- Signs of the Times: Graphic Design – 13:40

- Fashion Forward: Wardrobe and Styling – 20:40
- Screen Tests: Rachael and Pris – 8:54
- The Light That Burns: Remembering Jordan Cronenweth – 19:58
- Deleted & Alternate Scenes – 45:47
- Promoting Dystopia: Rendering the Poster Art – 9:35
- Deck-A-Rep: The True Nature of Rick Deckard – 9:30
- Nexus Generation: Fans and Filmmakers – 21:49
- 1982 Promotional Featurettes – 36:21

Sequels

K.W. Jeter, a friend of Philip K. Dick, has written three official, authorised *Blade Runner* novels that continue Rick Deckard's story, attempting to resolve many differences between *Blade Runner* and the source novel *Do Androids Dream of Electric Sheep?*

- *Blade Runner 2: The Edge of Human* (1995)
- *Blade Runner 3: Replicant Night* (1996)
- *Blade Runner 4: Eye and Talon* (2000)

Ridley Scott apparently toyed with the idea of a sequel film, which would have been titled *Metropolis*. However, the project was ultimately shelved due to rights issues. A script was also written for a proposed sequel titled *Blade Runner Down*, which would have been based on K. W. Jeter's first *Blade Runner* sequel novel. At the 2007 Comic-Con, Scott again announced that he was considering a sequel to the film. *Eagle Eye* co-writer Travis Wright worked with producer Bud Yorke for a few years on the project. His colleague John Glenn, who left the film by 2008, stated the script explores the nature of the off-world colonies as well as what happens to the Tyrell Corporation in the wake of its founder's death.

Prequel

In June 2009, *The New York Times* reported that Ridley Scott, together with his brother Tony Scott, was working on a prequel to *Blade Runner*. The prequel, *Purefold*, will be a series of 5–10 minute shorts, aimed first at the web and then perhaps television, and will be set at a point in time before 2019. Due to rights issues, the series will not be linked too closely to the characters or events of the 1982 film.

Comics

Archie Goodwin scripted the comic book adaptation, *A Marvel Comics Super Special: Blade Runner*, published September 1982. The Jim Steranko cover leads into a 45-page adaptation illustrated by the team of Al Williamson, Carlos Garzon, Dan Green and Ralph Reese. This adaptation includes one possible explanation of the title's significance in story context: the narrative line, "Blade runner. You're always movin' on the edge".

In 2009, BOOM! Studios published a 24-issue miniseries comic book adaptation of the *Blade Runner* source novel, *Do Androids Dream of Electric Sheep?* In April 2010, Boom! Studios announced a follow up comic was in production. *Dust To Dust* will be a four issue miniseries starting on May 26, 2010 and will be written by Chris Robertson and drawn by Robert Adler.

Video games

Main articles: Blade Runner (1985 video game) and Blade Runner (1997 video game)

There are two video games based on the film, one for Commodore 64, Sinclair ZX Spectrum and Amstrad CPC (1985) by CRL Group PLC based on the music by Vangelis (due to licensing issues), and another action adventure PC game (1997) by Westwood Studios. The Westwood PC game featured new characters and branching storylines based on the *Blade Runner* world. Eldon Tyrell, Gaff, Leon, Rachael, Chew, and J.F. Sebastian are seen, and their voice files were recorded by the original actors. DNA Row, the Eye Works, the Police Headquarters, Howie Lee's, the Tyrell Corporation building, and J.F. Sebastian's hotel are faithfully replicated. The events portrayed in the 1997 game occur not after, but in parallel to those in the film. The player assumes the role of McCoy, another replicant-hunter working at the same time as Deckard. Although Deckard is seen in photo evidence and referred to in dialogue, Deckard and McCoy never meet, preserving the canon of the film and the independence of the game plot.

The PC game featured a non-linear plot, non-player characters that each ran in their own independent AI, and an unusual pseudo-3D engine (which eschewed polygonal solids in favor of voxel elements) that did not require the use of a 3D accelerator card to play the game.

A prototype board game was also created in California (1982) that had game play similar to *Scotland Yard*.

Television series

Main article: Total Recall 2070

Though not an official sequel to *Blade Runner*, *Total Recall 2070* was initially planned as a spin-off of the movie *Total Recall* but transformed into a hybrid of that movie and *Blade Runner*. There are many similarities between the television series and the *Blade Runner* universe. The series takes place in a dark, crowded, industrial, and cosmopolitan setting. David Hume is a senior detective for the Citizens Protection Bureau (CPB) who is partnered with Ian Farve, an Alpha Class android. The series focused on questions such as the nature of humanity and the rights of androids. The series was based on two works by Philip K. Dick: "We Can Remember It for You Wholesale" (the basis for the film *Total Recall*), and *Do Androids Dream of Electric Sheep?* (the basis for *Blade Runner*).

External links

- Official website [1]
- Off-world: The *Blade Runner* Wiki [4]
- *Blade Runner* [2] at the Internet Movie Database
- *Blade Runner* [3] at Allmovie
- *Blade Runner* [4] at the TCM Movie Database
- *Blade Runner* [5] at Rotten Tomatoes
- *Blade Runner* [6] at Box Office Mojo
- Blade Runner [7] at the Open Directory Project
- BRmovie [8]

Dr. Richard Kimble

Richard Kimble

Dr. Richard David Kimble is the fictional character featured in the hit television series *The Fugitive*, portrayed by actor David Janssen. Kimble is a pediatrician falsely convicted for the murder of his wife, Helen Kimble, but freed in a train wreck en route to execution. He spends the series searching for the one-armed man, Fred Johnson, who is the real killer; while pursued by the relentless police detective, Lt. Philip Gerard, from whom he escaped. This style of show (traveling from town-to-town and the constant changing of identities/names) was the prototype for many later American TV series such as *Alias Smith and Jones*, *The Incredible Hulk* and *Renegade*.

The character was also featured in the 1993 film *The Fugitive,* based loosely on the original series, starring Harrison Ford and Tommy Lee Jones as a United States marshal in pursuit of him. In the film version, Kimble was a prominent Chicago vascular surgeon rather than a small-town pediatrician. This change was necessary to support the plot change in which the killing of Kimble's wife was not a senseless murder by a transient during a botched robbery attempt (as in the original series) but rather the result of a fiendish plot by an evil drug company executive.

Yet a third incarnation of Richard Kimble surfaced in an updated remake of the original *Fugitive* series which aired during the 2000-2001 television season. Kimble in this version was portrayed by actor Timothy Daly, whose father James had guest starred in two segments of the original series.

The Fugitive (1993 film)

The Fugitive	
Theatrical release poster	
Directed by	Andrew Davis
Produced by	Arnold Kopelson
Written by	Jeb Stuart (Screenplay) David Twohy (Story and screenplay) Roy Huggins (Characters)
Starring	Harrison Ford Tommy Lee Jones
Music by	James Newton Howard
Cinematography	Michael Chapman
Editing by	Dennis Virkler
Distributed by	Warner Bros.
Release date(s)	August 6, 1993
Running time	130 minutes
Country	United States
Language	English
Budget	$44,000,000
Gross revenue	$368,700,000
Followed by	*U.S. Marshals*

The Fugitive is a 1993 American film based on the television series of the same name. The film was directed by Andrew Davis and stars Harrison Ford and Tommy Lee Jones. Jones won an Academy Award for Best Supporting Actor for his performance. The supporting cast includes Andreas Katsulas, Sela Ward, Jeroen Krabbé, Julianne Moore, and Joe Pantoliano. The film was one of the few movies associated with a television series to be nominated for the Academy Award for Best Picture.

Plot

Dr. Richard Kimble, a successful surgeon in Chicago, comes home one night to find his wife Helen fatally wounded by a one-armed man, and though he attempts to subdue the killer, the man escapes. The lack of evidence of a break-in, being the beneficiary of Helen's lucrative life insurance and a misunderstood 9-1-1 call lead to Kimble being convicted of first-degree murder, for which he is sentenced to death. On his way to death row via bus, the other prisoners attempt an escape that wounds a guard and kills the driver, causing the bus to fall into the path of an oncoming train. Kimble barely escapes the bus's destruction—saving the guard's life by dragging him out of the bus—and flees into the night. The United States Marshals arrive, led by Samuel Gerard, to locate and round up the escaped convicts while the injured are taken to a nearby hospital. Kimble sneaks into the same hospital to dispose of his prison uniform, shave his beard, and treat his wounds. While leaving the hospital, he is recognized by the injured guard, but quickly drives away in an ambulance. Gerard blockades the tunnel through a nearby dam to stop Kimble's escape, but Kimble abandons the vehicle and climbs into the storm water system. Kimble is eventually cornered by Gerard above the outlet of the dam spillway. Kimble dives over the edge and swims away downstream, leaving no trail for the Marshals to follow.

Kimble returns to Chicago to find the murderer and receives some money from his friend and associate, Dr. Charles Nichols. Posing as a janitor, Kimble enters Cook County Hospital's prosthetic department to obtain a list of people who had their prosthetic arm repaired shortly after his wife's murder. Gerard realizes that Kimble must be looking for the one-armed man and begins a similar search to anticipate Kimble's next move. Kimble goes to the Cook County Jail to meet a one-armed man accused of armed robbery, but sees he is not the murderer. Gerard and his team also go to the jail with the same suspicion, and Gerard spots Kimble as he is leaving. A chase ensues, in which Gerard fires several shots at Kimble which are stopped by bulletproof glass. Gerard chases Kimble into Chicago's St. Patrick's Day parade where Kimble barely escapes. At the home of the next person on the list, a former police officer named Frederick Sykes, Kimble confirms the man is the murderer and finds he is employed by a pharmaceutical company that is working on a new drug called Provasic. Kimble had investigated the drug and discovered that it caused liver damage, which would have prevented it from being approved by the FDA. He also finds that Nichols, who is leading the drug's development, arranged a cover-up, and ordered Sykes to kill Kimble (his wife's death was incidental). Gerard follows Kimble to Sykes's home and draws the same conclusion.

As Kimble takes an L Train to confront Nichols, Sykes attacks him, and in the ensuing struggle, Sykes shoots a transit cop before being subdued and handcuffed to a wall by Kimble. Moments later, Kimble interrupts Nichols's speech, accusing him of falsifying his data. They begin to fight while being chased by Gerard and hostile Chicago police. When Kimble, Nichols, and Gerard are all in the hotel's laundry room, Gerard calls out that he knows about the conspiracy organized by Nichols. Hearing this, Nichols turns to shoot Gerard but at the last moment Kimble hits him from behind, saving Gerard's life. Kimble is taken into custody, since he was still technically a fugitive. Once inside the car Gerard unlocks his handcuffs as they are driven away.

Cast

- Harrison Ford as Dr. Richard Kimble
- Tommy Lee Jones as Deputy Samuel Gerard
- Jeroen Krabbé as Dr. Charles Nichols
- Andreas Katsulas as Frederick Sykes
- Joe Pantoliano as Agent Cosmo Renfro
- Sela Ward as Helen Kimble
- Julianne Moore as Dr. Anne Eastman
- Daniel Roebuck as Agent Robert Biggs
- L. Scott Caldwell as Agent Poole
- Tom Wood as Agent Noah Newman
- Ron Dean as Detective Kelly
- Joseph F. Kosala as Detective Rosetti
- David Darlow as Dr. Lentz
- Eddie Bo Smith Jr. as Copeland
- Jane Lynch as Dr. Kathy Wahlund
- Nick Searcy as Sheriff Rawlins

Production

Although almost half of the film is set in rural Illinois, a large portion of the principal filming was actually shot in Jackson County, North Carolina in the Great Smoky Mountains. The famous scene involving Kimble's prison transport bus and a freight train wreck was filmed along the Great Smoky Mountains Railroad just outside of Dillsboro, North Carolina. Riders on the excursion railroad can still see the wreckage on the way out of the Dillsboro depot. Scenes in a hospital after Kimble's escape were filmed at Harris Regional Hospital in Sylva, North Carolina. Cheoah Dam was the location of the scene where Kimble jumped. In one scene, a road sign pointing to Murphy can be seen.

The rest of the film was shot in Chicago, Illinois, including some of the dam scenes, which were filmed in the remains of the Chicago freight tunnels (as well as Deals Gap, North Carolina). The "one-armed man" lived in the historic Pullman neighborhood of Chicago. Harrison Ford used the pay phone in the Pullman Pub, at which point he climbs a ladder and runs down the roofline of the historic rowhouses toward the one-armed man's house. There are several other scenes that show the rowhouses of the historic neighborhood. During the St. Patrick's Day Parade chase scene, Mayor Richard M. Daley and then-Illinois Attorney General Roland W. Burris are briefly shown as participants. One night scene under the "El" tracks showed Kimble exiting an alley by 130 N. Wells St., with "Chicago Memorial" covering the then-Illinois Bell Building sign.

Reception

The Fugitive opened strongly in the United States box office, grossing $23,758,855 in its first weekend and holding the top spot for six weeks until *Striking Distance* pushed it into 2nd place the seventh week of its release. It eventually went on to gross an estimated $183,875,760 in the US, and $368,700,000 worldwide.

The film was nominated for the following seven Academy Awards:

- Best Supporting Actor - Tommy Lee Jones (**won**)
- Best Picture (lost to *Schindler's List*)
- Best Cinematography (lost to *Schindler's List*)
- Best Sound Effects Editing (lost to *Jurassic Park*)
- Best Film Editing (lost to *Schindler's List*)
- Best Original Music Score (lost to *Schindler's List*)
- Best Sound (lost to *Jurassic Park*)

Jones also received numerous other awards for his role, including the Golden Globe Award for Best Supporting Actor - Motion Picture. Director Andrew Davis received "Best Director" nominations at that year's Golden Globe and Directors Guild of America Awards (but was not honored with a similar nomination at the Academy Awards).

It also received enthusiastic reviews from film critics. As of July 2009, it received a 94% score and has been certified "Fresh" on Rotten Tomatoes and a score of 86 or "universal acclaim" from Metacritic. Roger Ebert gave it 4 out of 4 stars, calling it "one of the year's best films". A few reviewers said it was marred by the ending, which introduced conspiracy and political elements to the film.

Novelization and remake

Jeanne Kalogridis wrote a mass-market paperback novelization of the film. She worked from the original screenplay, which eschews most of the humorous wisecracks spoken on film. Her novel looks more closely at some of the film's leading characters, especially Gerard and his newest subordinate. The film was also made into the Telugu film *Criminal* and the Malayalam film *Nirnayam*.

Sequel

Jones returned as Gerard in a sequel released in 1998, *U.S. Marshals*, which also featured Wesley Snipes, Robert Downey Jr., Joe Pantoliano, and Tom Wood. While the second film also features Gerard's team of marshals hunting down an escaped fugitive accused of murder, it does not involve Kimble or the events of the first film. However, the fictional hospital at which Kimble works, Chicago Memorial, is featured.

External links

- *The Fugitive* [1] at the Internet Movie Database
- *The Fugitive* [2] at Allmovie
- *The Fugitive* [3] at Rotten Tomatoes
- *The Fugitive* [4] at Box Office Mojo

Bob Falfa

American Graffiti

American Graffiti	
Film poster by Mort Drucker	
Directed by	George Lucas
Produced by	Francis Ford Coppola Gary Kurtz
Written by	George Lucas Gloria Katz Willard Huyck
Starring	Richard Dreyfuss Ron Howard Paul Le Mat Charles Martin Smith Cindy Williams Candy Clark Mackenzie Phillips Harrison Ford
Cinematography	Jan D'Alquen Ron Eveslage Haskell Wexler
Editing by	Verna Fields Marcia Lucas
Studio	Universal Pictures Lucasfilm The Coppola Company
Distributed by	Universal Pictures
Release date(s)	**Original:** August 11, 1973 **Reissue:** May 1978

Running time	**1973:** 108 min. **1978 Reissue & Home video:** 112 min.
Country	United States
Language	English
Budget	$775,000
Gross revenue	$118 million
Followed by	*More American Graffiti*

American Graffiti is a 1973 coming of age comedy-drama film co-written and directed by George Lucas, and starring Richard Dreyfuss, Ron Howard, Paul Le Mat, Charles Martin Smith, Cindy Williams, Candy Clark, Mackenzie Phillips, Bo Hopkins, Kathleen Quinlan and Harrison Ford. Set in Modesto, California, *American Graffiti* is a study of the cruising and rock and roll cultures popular among the Post-World War II baby boom generation. The film is a nostalgic portrait of teenage life in the early 1960s told in a series of vignettes, featuring a group of teenagers and their adventures in a single night in late August 1962.

The genesis of *American Graffiti* was in Lucas's own teenage years in early 1960s Modesto. He was unsuccessful in pitching the concept to financiers and distributors, but finally found favor at Universal Pictures after United Artists, 20th Century Fox, Columbia Pictures, Metro-Goldwyn-Mayer, and Paramount Pictures turned him down. Filming was initially set to take place in San Rafael, California, but the production crew was denied permission to shoot beyond a second day. As a result, most filming for *American Graffiti* was conducted in Petaluma.

American Graffiti was released to universal critical acclaim and financial success, and was nominated for the Academy Award for Best Picture. Produced and marketed on a $775,000 budget, the film has turned out to be one of the most profitable movies of all time. Since its initial release, *American Graffiti* has garnered an estimated return of well over $200 million in box office gross and home video sales, not including merchandising. In 1995, the United States Library of Congress deemed the film culturally significant and selected it for preservation in the National Film Registry.

Plot

The film opens in the early evening sometime in late August, 1962. Recent high school graduates and longtime friends Curt Henderson and Steve Bolander, meet up with friends Terry "The Toad" Fields and John Milner at the local Mel's Drive-In parking lot. Despite receiving a $2,000 scholarship, Curt is undecided if he wants to leave the next morning with Steve to go to the Northeastern United States to begin college. Steve lets Toad borrow his 1958 Chevy Impala for the evening and while he will be away at college. Steve's girlfriend Laurie, who is also Curt's younger sister, is unsure of Steve leaving, to which he suggests they see other people while he is away to "strengthen" their relationship. During the night at Mel's, Milner sees a black 1955 Chevy. Curt implies the Chevy's driver is someone wishing to challenge John to a race.

Curt, Steve and Laurie go to the local sock hop, while Toad and Milner begin cruising. En route to the hop, Curt sees a beautiful blonde girl (Suzanne Somers) in a white 1956 Ford Thunderbird. She mouths "I love you" before disappearing down the street and Curt is aroused and spends the rest of the film searching for her. After leaving the hop, Curt is desperate to find the mysterious blonde, but is stopped by a group of greasers ("The Pharaohs") through an initiation rite that involves hooking a chain to a police car and successfully ripping out its rear axle. Curt is told rumors that "The Blonde" is either a trophy wife or prostitute, which he immediately refuses to accept.

Steve and Laurie break up after a series of arguments, and Milner inadvertently picks up Carol, an annoying teenybopper. Toad, who is normally socially inept with girls, meets a flirtatious and rebellious girl named Debbie (Candy Clark) who convinces Toad to get her alcohol. Meanwhile, Curt learns that DJ Wolfman Jack broadcasts from just outside of Modesto, and inside the dark, eerie radio station, Curt encounters a bearded man who claims only to be the manager. Curt hands the man a message for the blonde to call him or meet him. As he walks away, Curt sees the "manager" performing into the on air mic and realizes he had been speaking with the DJ the whole time.

The other story lines intertwine until Toad and Steve end up on "Paradise Road" to watch Milner race his deuce coupe against the arrogant Bob Falfa (Harrison Ford) in his 55 Chevy, with Laurie as Falfa's passenger. Within seconds Falfa loses control of his car and plunges into a ditch. Steve and Milner run to the wreck, and a dazed Bob and Laurie stagger out of the car before it explodes. Distraught, Laurie grips Steve tightly and tells him not to leave her. He assures her that he has decided not to leave Modesto after all. The next morning, Curt is awakened by the sound of a phone ringing in a telephone booth, which turns out to be the blonde. She tells him she might see him cruising tonight, but Curt replies that is not possible, because he will be leaving. At the airfield, he says goodbye to his parents, his sister and friends. As the DC-7 airliner takes off, Curt gazes out of the window, seeing the white Ford Thunderbird, which belongs to the mysterious blonde, heading out of town in the same direction as his plane.

Prior to the end credits, an on-screen epilogue reveals that John was killed by a drunk driver in December 1964, Terry was reported missing in action near An Lộc in December 1965, Steve is an insurance agent in Modesto, California, and Curt is a writer living in Canada.

Cast

- Richard Dreyfuss as Curt Henderson
- Ronny Howard as Steve Bolander
- Paul Le Mat as John Milner
- Charles Martin Smith as Terry "The Toad" Fields
- Cindy Williams as Laurie Henderson
- Candy Clark as Debbie Dunham
- Mackenzie Phillips as Carol Morrison
- Harrison Ford as Bob Falfa
- Bo Hopkins as Joe Young
- Wolfman Jack as XERB Disc Jockey
- Kathleen Quinlan as Peg
- Manuel Padilla, Jr. and Beau Gentry as Carlos and Ants
- Jim Bohan as Officer Holstein
- Jana Bellan as Budda
- Flash Cadillac & the Continental Kids as Herbie and the Heartbeats
- Suzanne Somers as Blonde in T-Bird
- Deby Celiz as Wendy
- Lynne Marie Stewart as Bobbie Tucker

Development

Inspiration

During the production of *THX 1138* (1971), producer Francis Ford Coppola challenged co-writer/director George Lucas to write a script that would appeal to mainstream audiences. Lucas embraced the idea, using his early 1960s teenage experiences cruising in Modesto, California. "Cruising was gone, and I felt compelled to document the whole experience and what my generation used as a way of meeting girls," Lucas explained. As he developed the story in his mind, Lucas included his fascination with Wolfman Jack. Lucas had considered doing a documentary about The Wolfman when he attended the USC School of Cinematic Arts, but dropped the idea.

Adding in semi-autobiographical connotations, Lucas set the story in 1962 Modesto. The characters Curt Henderson, John Milner and Terry "The Toad" Fields also represent different stages from his younger life. Curt is modeled after Lucas's personality during USC, while Milner is based on Lucas's teenage drag racing and junior college years, and hot rod enthusiasts he had known from the Kustom Kulture in Modesto. Toad represents Lucas's nerd years as a freshman in high school, specifically his "bad luck" with dating. The filmmaker was also inspired by Federico Fellini's *I Vitelloni* (1953).

United Artists

After Warner Bros. abandoned Lucas's early version of *Apocalypse Now* (1979) (during the post-production of *THX 1138*), the filmmaker decided to continue development on *Another Quiet Night in Modesto*, which he eventually changed to *American Graffiti*. To co-write a fifteen-page film treatment, Lucas hired Willard Huyck and Gloria Katz, who also added semi-autobiographical connotations to the storyline. In attempting to use the treatment to attract financing, Lucas and producer Gary Kurtz began pitching *American Graffiti* to various Hollywood studios and production companies, but they were unsuccessful. Financiers believed music licensing issues would distract the film's budget. Alongside *Easy Rider* (1969), *American Graffiti* represents one of the first films to avoid a traditional film score approach and successfully rely on scenes specifically synchronized to an assortment of songs.

THX 1138 was released in March 1971 and Lucas was offered opportunities to direct *Lady Ice* (1973), *Tommy* (1975) or *Hair* (1979). He turned down the offers, determined to pursue his own projects, despite his desperation to find another film to direct. During this time, Lucas conceived the idea for an untitled space opera, which would later become the basis for his *Star Wars* franchise. At the May 1971 Cannes Film Festival, *THX* was chosen for the Directors' Fortnight competition. There, Lucas met David Picker, then president of United Artists, who was intrigued by *American Graffiti* and Lucas's as-yet-untitled space opera. Picker decided to give Lucas $10,000 to develop *Graffiti* as a screenplay.

Lucas intended to spend another five weeks in Europe and hoped that Huyck and Katz would have a screenplay by the time he returned, but they were about to start on their own film, *Messiah of Evil* (1972), so Lucas hired Richard Walter, a colleague from the USC School of Cinematic Arts. Walter was flattered, but instead tried to pitch Lucas a screenplay called *Barry and the Persuasions*, a story of East Coast teenagers in the late 1950s. Lucas held firm - his was a story about West Coast teenagers in the early 1960s. Walter was paid the $10,000, and he began to adapt the Lucas/Huyck/Katz treatment into a screenplay.

Lucas was dismayed when he returned to America in June 1971 and read Walter's script, which was written in the style and tone of an exploitation film. "It was overtly sexual and very fantasy-like, with playing chicken and things that kids didn't really do," Lucas reasoned. "I wanted something that was more like the way I grew up." Walter's script also had Steve and Laurie going to Nevada to get married without their parents' permission. He redrafted the screenplay, but Lucas fired Walter over creative differences.

After paying Walter, Lucas had exhausted his development fund with United Artists. He began writing the script, completing his first draft in just three weeks. Drawing upon his large collection of vintage records, Lucas wrote every scene with a musical backdrop in mind. The cost of licensing the 75 songs Lucas wanted was a contributing factor in United Artists' ultimate rejection of the script, which the studio also felt was too experimental - "a musical montage with no characters." United Artists also passed on *Star Wars*, which Lucas shelved for the time being.

Universal Pictures

Lucas spent the rest of 1971 and early 1972 trying to raise financing for the *American Graffiti* script. During this time, 20th Century Fox, Columbia Pictures, Metro-Goldwyn-Mayer and Paramount Pictures all turned down the opportunity to co-finance and distribute the film. Lucas, Huyck and Katz rewrote the second draft together, which, in addition to Modesto, was also set in Mill Valley and Los Angeles. Lucas also intended to end *American Graffiti* showing a title card detailing the fate of the characters, including the death of Milner and the disappearance of Toad in Vietnam. Huyck and Katz found the ending depressing and were incredulous that Lucas planned to include only the male characters. Lucas argued that mentioning the girls meant adding another title card, which he felt would prolong the ending. Because of this, Pauline Kael later accused Lucas of chauvinism.

Lucas and producer Gary Kurtz took the script to American International Pictures, who expressed interest, but ultimately believed *American Graffiti* was not violent or sexual enough for the studio's standards. Lucas and Kurtz eventually found favor at Universal Pictures, who allowed Lucas total artistic control and the right of final cut privilege on the condition that he make *American Graffiti* on a strict, low budget. This forced Lucas to drop the opening scene, in which the Blonde Angel, Curt's image of the perfect woman, drives through an empty drive-in cinema in her Ford Thunderbird, her transparency revealing she does not exist.

Universal initially projected a $600,000 budget, but added an additional $175,000 once producer Francis Ford Coppola signed on. This would allow the studio to advertise *American Graffiti* as "from the Man who Gave you *The Godfather* (1972)." However, Lucas was forced to concede final cut privilege. The proposition also gave Universal first look deals on Lucas's next two planned projects, *Star Wars* (1977) and *Radioland Murders* (1994). As he continued to work on the script, Lucas encountered difficulties on the Steve and Laurie storyline. Lucas, Katz and Huyck worked on the third draft together, specifically on the scenes featuring Steve and Laurie.

Production proceeded with virtually no input or interference from Universal. *American Graffiti* was a low-budget film, and executive Ned Tanen had only modest expectations of its commercial success. However, Universal did object to the film's title, not knowing what "American Graffiti" meant; Lucas was dismayed when some executives assumed he was making an Italian movie about feet. The studio therefore submitted a long list of over 60 alternative titles, with their favorite being *Another Slow Night in Modesto* and Coppola's *Rock Around the Block*. They pushed hard to get Lucas to adopt any of the titles, but he was displeased with all the alternatives and persuaded Tanen to keep *American Graffiti*.

Production

Casting

The film's lengthy casting process was overseen by Fred Roos, who worked with producer Francis Ford Coppola on *The Godfather*. Because *American Graffiti*'s main cast was associated with younger actors, the casting call and notices went through numerous high school drama groups and community theaters in the San Francisco Bay Area. Among the actors was Mark Hamill, the future Luke Skywalker in Lucas' *Star Wars* trilogy.

Over 100 unknown actors auditioned for Curt Henderson before Richard Dreyfuss was cast. George Lucas was impressed with Dreyfuss' thoughtful analysis of the role, and, as a result, offered the actor his choosing of Curt or Terry "The Toad" Fields. Roos, a former casting director on *The Andy Griffith Show*, suggested Ron Howard for Steve Bolander. Howard reluctantly accepted the part in attempting to avoid his typecasting as a child actor. Bob Balaban turned down The Toad out of fear of typecasting, a decision which he later regretted. Charles Martin Smith was eventually cast in the role.

Although Cindy Williams was cast as Laurie Henderson, the actress hoped she would get the part of Debbie Dunham, which ended up going to Candy Clark. Mackenzie Phillips, who portrays Carol, was only 12 years old, and under California law, producer Gary Kurtz had to become her legal guardian during filming. As Bob Falfa, Roos cast Harrison Ford, who was then concentrating on a carpentry career. Ford agreed to take the role on the condition that he would not have to cut his hair. The character has a flattop haircut in the script, but a compromise was eventually reached whereby Ford wore a stetson to cover his hair. Producer Francis Ford Coppola encouraged Lucas to cast Wolfman Jack as himself in a cameo appearance. "George Lucas and I went through thousands of Wolfman Jack phone calls that were taped with the public," Jack reflected. "The telephone calls [heard on the broadcasts] in the motion picture and on the soundtrack were actual calls with real people."

Filming

Although *American Graffiti* is set in 1962 Modesto, California, Lucas believed the city had changed too much in 10 years and initially chose San Rafael as the primary shooting location. Filming began on June 26, 1972, however, Lucas soon became frustrated at the time it was taking to fix camera mounts to the cars. A key member of the production had also been arrested for growing marijuana, and, in addition to already running behind the shooting schedule, the San Rafael City Council immediately became concerned about the disruption that filming caused for local businesses and had therefore withdrawn permission to shoot beyond a second day.

Petaluma, a similarly small town approximately 20 miles north of San Rafael, became more cooperative and *American Graffiti* moved there without the loss of a single day of shooting. Lucas convinced the San Rafael City Council to allow two further nights of filming for general cruising shots, which he used to evoke as much of the intended location as possible in the finished film. Shooting in

Petaluma began on June 28 and proceeded at a quick pace. Lucas mimicked the filmmaking style of B movie producer Sam Katzman in attempting to save money and authenticated low budget filming methods.

In addition to Petaluma, other locations included Van Ness Avenue in San Francisco, Sonoma, Richmond, Novato and the Buchanan Field Airport in Concord. More problems ensued during filming. Paul Le Mat was sent to the hospital after an allergic reaction to walnuts. Actors Le Mat, Harrison Ford and Bo Hopkins were often drunk between takes and had conducted climbing competitions to the top of the local Holiday Inn sign. One actor set fire to Lucas' motel room. Another night, Le Mat threw Richard Dreyfuss into a swimming pool, gashing his forehead on the day before he was due to have his close-ups filmed. Dreyfuss also complained over the wardrobe that Lucas had chosen for the character. Ford was arrested one night while in a bar fight and kicked out of his motel room. In addition, two camera operators were nearly killed when filming the climactic race scene on Frates Rd outside Petaluma. Principal photography ended on August 4, 1972.

Cinematography

Lucas considered covering duties as the sole cinematographer, but dropped the idea. Instead, he elected to shoot *American Graffiti* using two cinematographers (as he had done in *THX 1138*) and no formal director of photography. Two cameras were used simultaneously in scenes involving conversations between actors in different cars, which resulted in significant production time savings. After CinemaScope proved to be too expensive, Lucas decided that *American Graffiti* should have a documentary-like feel, and shot the film using Techniscope cameras. He believed that Techniscope, an inexpensive way of shooting in 35 mm film and utilizing only half of the film's frame, would give a perfect widescreen format resembling 16 mm. Adding to the documentary feel was Lucas's openness for the cast to improvise scenes. He also used goofs for the final cut, notably Charles Martin Smith's (Toad) arriving on his scooter to meet Steve outside Mel's Drive-In. Jan D'Alquen and Ron Eveslage were hired as the cinematographers, but filming with Techniscope cameras brought lighting problems. As a result, Lucas commissioned help from friend Haskell Wexler, who was credited as the "visual consultant".

Editing

Lucas wanted to have wife Marcia edit *American Graffiti*, but Universal executive Ned Tanen insisted on Verna Fields, who had just finished Steven Spielberg's *The Sugarland Express* (1974). Fields worked on the first rough cut of the film before she left to resume work on *What's Up, Doc?* (1972). Following Fields's departure, Lucas struggled with editing the film's story structure. He had written the script so that the four (Curt, Steve, John and Toad) storylines were always presented in the same sequence. The first cut of *American Graffiti* was three-and-a-half hours long; and, in removing an hour and a half, numerous scenes were cut and many others were shortened and combined. The film became increasingly loose, with the result that the presentations of scenes no longer resembled Lucas's original "ABCD structure." At 112 minutes, Lucas completed his final cut of *American Graffiti* in December 1972. Walter Murch assisted Lucas in post-production for audio mixing and sound design purposes. Murch suggested making Wolfman Jack's radio show the "backbone" of the film. "The Wolfman was an ethereal presence in the lives of young people," said producer Gary Kurtz, "and it was that quality we wanted and obtained in the picture."

Soundtrack

Main article: 41 Original Hits from the Soundtrack of American Graffiti

Universal wanted Lucas and producer Gary Kurtz to hire an orchestra for sound-alikes. The studio eventually proposed a flat deal that offered every music publisher the same amount of money. This was acceptable to most of the companies representing Lucas's first choices, but not to RCA - with the consequence that Elvis Presley is conspicuously absent from the soundtrack. "I used the absence of music, and sound effects, to create the drama," Lucas later explained. In any event, '50s and '60s music (ranging from Bill Haley and His Comets to The Beach Boys) provides the film's score. All home video versions contain the entirety of this music with no changes or rescore.

Reception

Release

Despite unanimous positive praise at a January 1973 test screening, which was attended by Universal executive Ned Tanen, the studio threatened to re-edit *American Graffiti* from George Lucas's original cut. Lucas and producer Francis Ford Coppola began conflicting with Universal, to which Coppola offered to literally "buy the film" from the studio, insisting he was prepared to reimburse Universal's $775,000 budget. 20th Century Fox and Paramount Pictures also gave similar offers to the studio. The conflicts between Lucas and Universal only led to the studio threatening to have William Hornbeck completely re-edit *American Graffiti.*

When Coppola's *The Godfather* (1972) won the Academy Award for Best Picture in March 1973, Universal decided to cut only three scenes (about four minutes) from Lucas's cut. This included Toad's encounter with a fast-talking car salesman, an argument between Steve and his former teacher Mr. Kroot at the sock hop, and Bob Falfa's effort to serenade Laurie with "Some Enchanted Evening". However, Universal believed that *American Graffiti*, in its edited form, was only fit for release as a television movie.

Positive word of mouth came from various employees at Universal and the studio dropped the TV movie idea and began securing theaters in Los Angeles and New York for a limited release. However, Universal presidents Sidney Sheinberg and Lew Wasserman found out about the critical praise in LA and New York, and the marketing department rejuvenated their promotion strategy for *American Graffiti*, by investing an additional $500,000 in marketing and promotion. The film was released in the United States on August 1, 1973 to sleeper hit reception. *American Graffiti*, which cost $1.27 million to produce/market, yielded a worldwide box office gross that topped $55 million. Outside America, however, the film had only modest success, but acquired cult film recognition in France.

Universal reissued *Graffiti* in 1978 and earned an additional $63 million, totalling $118 million for the two releases. The reissue included stereophonic sound, and the additional four minutes that the studio had removed from Lucas's original cut. All home video releases also included these scenes. At the end of its theatrical run, *American Graffiti* had one of the lowest cost-to-profit ratios of a motion picture ever. Producer Francis Ford Coppola regretted having not financed the film himself. Lucas recalled, "He would have made $30 million on the deal. He never got over it and he still kicks himself." It was the thirteenth-highest grossing film of all time in 1977, and, adjusted for inflation, is currently the forty-third highest. By the 1990s, *American Graffiti* had earned more than $200 million in box office gross and home video sales. In December 1997 *Variety* reported that the film had earned an additional $55.13 million in rental revenue.

Universal Studios Home Entertainment first released the film on DVD in September 1998, and once more as a double feature with *More American Graffiti* (1979) in January 2004.

Aside from the four minutes originally deleted from Lucas' original cut retained, the only major change in the DVD version is the main title sequence, particularly the sky background to Mel's Drive-In, which was redone by ILM.

Critical analysis

American Graffiti went on to receive universal critical acclaim. Based on 33 reviews collected by *Rotten Tomatoes*, 97% of the critics enjoyed the film with an average score of 8.3/10. The consensus reads: "One of the most influential of all teen films, *American Graffiti* is a funny, nostalgic, and bittersweet look at a group of recent high school grads' last days of innocence." Roger Ebert praised the film for being "not only a great movie but a brilliant work of historical fiction; no sociological treatise could duplicate the movie's success in remembering exactly how it was to be alive at that cultural instant."

Jay Cocks of *Time* magazine wrote that *American Graffiti* "reveals a new and welcome depth of feeling. Few films have shown quite so well the eagerness, the sadness, the ambitions and small defeats of a generation of young Americans." A.D. Murphy from *Variety* felt *American Graffiti* was a vivid "recall of teenage attitudes and morals, told with outstanding empathy and compassion through an exceptionally talented cast of unknown actors." Dave Kehr, writing in the *Chicago Reader*, called the film a brilliant work of popular art that redefined nostalgia as a marketable commodity, while establishing a new narrative style.

Themes

The 1962 setting represents an end of an era in American society and pop culture. The musical backdrop also links between the early years of rock and roll in the mid-late 1950s (i.e. Bill Haley & His Comets, Elvis Presley and Buddy Holly) and the early 1960s British Invasion. The setting is also before the outbreaks of the Vietnam War and the John F. Kennedy assassination. *American Graffiti* evokes mankind's relationship with machines, notably the elaborate number of hot rods and teenagers' obsession with radio. The inclusion of Wolfman Jack also adds a mysterious and mythological analysis of teenage life in 1962. *American Graffiti* depicts multiple characters going through a coming of age, such as the decisions to attend college or reside in a small town.

Awards

American Graffiti was nominated for the Academy Award for Best Picture, but lost to *The Sting* (1973). Further nominations at the 46th Academy Awards included Best Director (George Lucas), Best Original Screenplay (Lucas, Willard Huyck and Gloria Katz), Best Supporting Actress (Candy Clark) and Best Film Editing (Verna Fields and Marcia Lucas). The film won Best Motion Picture (Musical or Comedy) at the 31st Golden Globe Awards, while Paul Le Mat won Most Promising Newcomer. Lucas was nominated for Best Director and Richard Dreyfuss was nominated for Best Actor in a Comedy or Musical. More nominations included Cindy Williams by the British Academy of Film and Television Arts for Best Actress in a Supporting Role, Lucas for the Directors Guild of America Award for Outstanding Directing, and Lucas, Huyck and Katz by the Writers Guild of America for Best Original Comedy.

Legacy

Internet reviewer MaryAnn Johanson acknowledged that *American Graffiti* rekindled public and entertainment interest in the 1950s and '60s, and influenced other films such as *The Lords of Flatbush* (1974) and *Cooley High* (1975) and the TV series *Happy Days*. Alongside other films from the New Hollywood era, *American Graffiti* is often cited for helping give birth to the summer blockbuster. The film's box office success made George Lucas an instant millionaire. He gave an amount of the film's profits to Haskell Wexler for his visual consulting help during filming, and to Wolfman Jack for "inspiration". Lucas's net worth was now $4 million, and he set aside a $300,000 independent fund for his long cherished space opera project, which would eventually become the basis for *Star Wars* (1977).

The financial success of *Graffiti* also gave Lucas opportunities to establish more elaborate development for Lucasfilm, Skywalker Sound, and Industrial Light & Magic. Based on the success of the 1977 reissue, Universal began production for the sequel *More American Graffiti* (1979). Lucas and writers Willard Huyck and Gloria Katz later collaborated on *Radioland Murders* (1994), also released by Universal Pictures, for which Lucas acted as executive producer. The film features characters intended to be Curt and Laurie Henderson's parents, Roger and Penny Henderson. In 1995 *American Graffiti* was deemed culturally, historically, or aesthetically significant by the United States Library of Congress and selected for preservation in the National Film Registry. In 1997 the city of Modesto, California honored Lucas with a statue dedication of *American Graffiti* at George Lucas Plaza.

In 1998 the American Film Institute (AFI) ranked it as the seventy-seventh greatest film ever in the 100 Years... 100 Movies list. When the 10th Anniversary Edition came in June 2007, AFI moved *American Graffiti* to the sixty-second greatest film. The movie was also listed as the forty-third funniest. Director David Fincher credited *American Graffiti* as a visual influence for *Fight Club* (1999). Lucas's *Star Wars Episode II: Attack of the Clones* (2002) features references to the film. The yellow airspeeder that Anakin Skywalker and Obi-Wan Kenobi use to pursue the bounty hunter Zam Wesell is based on John Milner's yellow deuce coupe, while Dex's Diner is reminiscent of Mel's Drive-In. Adam Savage and Jamie Hyneman of *MythBusters* conducted the "rear axle" experiment on the January 11, 2004 episode.

Given the popularity of the film's cars with customizers and hot rodders in the years since its release, their fate immediately after the film is ironic. All were offered for sale in San Francisco newspaper ads; only the '58 Impala (driven by Ron Howard) attracted a buyer, selling for only a few hundred dollars. The yellow Deuce and the white T-bird went unsold, despite being priced as low as US$3,000. The registration plate on Milner's yellow deuce coupe is THX 138 on a yellow California license plate, slightly altered, reflecting Lucas's earlier science fiction film success.

References

- John Baxter (1999). *Mythmaker: The Life and Work of George Lucas*. New York City: Spike Books. ISBN 0-380-97833-4.
- Marcus Hearn (2005). *The Cinema of George Lucas*. New York City: ABRAMS Books. ISBN 0-8109-4968-7.
- Dale Pollock (1999). *Skywalking: The Life and Films of George Lucas*. New York City: Da Capo Press. ISBN 0-306-80904-4.

External links

- Official website [1]
- *American Graffiti* [2] at the Internet Movie Database
- *American Graffiti* [3] at Allmovie
- *American Graffiti* [4] at Rotten Tomatoes
- *American Graffiti* [5] at Box Office Mojo
- *American Graffiti* [6] at Filmsite.org
- The City of Petaluma's Salute to *American Graffiti* [7]

Colonel Lucas

Apocalypse Now

Apocalypse Now	
theatrical release poster by Bob Peak	
Directed by	Francis Ford Coppola
Produced by	Francis Ford Coppola
Screenplay by	John Milius Francis Ford Coppola
Story by	Joseph Conrad (novel)
Narrated by	Joe Estevez (*uncredited*)
Starring	Martin Sheen Marlon Brando Robert Duvall Laurence Fishburne Dennis Hopper Harrison Ford Frederic Forrest Sam Bottoms Albert Hall
Music by	Carmine Coppola Francis Ford Coppola
Cinematography	Vittorio Storaro
Editing by	Richard Marks Gerald B. Greenberg Walter Murch Lisa Fruchtman
Studio	American Zoetrope
Distributed by	United Artists
Release date(s)	August 15, 1979
Running time	153 minutes
Country	United States
Language	English

Budget	$31.5 million
Gross revenue	$78,784,010 *(1979)* $83,471,511 *(2002)*

Apocalypse Now is a 1979 American epic war film set during the Vietnam War. The plot revolves around two US Army special operations officers, one of whom, Captain Benjamin L. Willard (Martin Sheen) of MACV-SOG, is sent into the jungle to assassinate the other, the rogue and presumably insane Colonel Walter E. Kurtz (Marlon Brando) of Special Forces. The film was produced and directed by Francis Ford Coppola from a script by Coppola and John Milius. The script is based on Joseph Conrad's novella *Heart of Darkness*, and also draws elements from Michael Herr's *Dispatches*, the film version of Conrad's *Lord Jim* (which shares the same character of Marlow with *Heart of Darkness*), and Werner Herzog's *Aguirre, the Wrath of God* (1972).

The film became notorious in the entertainment press due to its lengthy and troubled production, as documented in *Hearts of Darkness: A Filmmaker's Apocalypse*. Marlon Brando showed up to the set overweight and Martin Sheen suffered a heart attack. The production was also beset by extreme weather that destroyed several expensive sets. In addition, the release date of the film was delayed several times as Coppola struggled to come up with an ending and to edit the millions of feet of footage that he had shot. The film won the Palme d'Or at Cannes and was nominated for the Academy Award for Best Picture and the Golden Globe Award for Best Motion Picture – Drama.

Plot

Act I

The film opens, introducing Captain Benjamin L. Willard (Martin Sheen); a deeply troubled, seasoned special operations veteran. It is 1969. Willard has returned to Saigon from deployment in the field. He drinks excessively and appears to be having difficulty adjusting to life in the rear-area. Two intelligence officers, Lt. General Corman (G. D. Spradlin) and Colonel Lucas (Harrison Ford), and a government man (Jerry Ziesmer) approach him with an assignment: journey up the fictitious Nung River into the remote Cambodian jungle to find Colonel Walter E. Kurtz (Marlon Brando), a member of the US Army Special Forces feared to have gone rogue.

They tell Willard that Kurtz, once considered a model officer and future general, has gone insane and is commanding a legion of his own Montagnard troops deep inside the forest in neutral Cambodia. Their claims are supported by very disturbing radio broadcasts and recordings made by Kurtz himself. Willard is ordered to undertake a mission to find Kurtz and terminate the Colonel's command "with extreme prejudice."

Willard joins the crew of a Navy Patrol Boat, Riverine (PBR), with an eclectic crew composed of: boat commander QMC George "Chief" Phillips (Albert Hall), GM3 Lance B. Johnson (Sam Bottoms), GM3 Tyrone Miller (Laurence Fishburne) a.k.a. "Mr. Clean", and EN3 Jay "Chef" Hicks (Frederic Forrest).

Willard and the PBR crew rendezvous with the 1/9 Air Cavalry, commanded by Lieutenant Colonel Bill Kilgore (Robert Duvall) for transport to the Nung River. He initially refuses their request for transport until Kilgore, a keen surfer, is told by one of his men that Lance Johnson, a professional surfer, is a member of the boat's crew. Kilgore befriends Johnson, and later learns from one of his men that the beach down the coast which marks the opening to the river is perfect for surfing. This changes Kilgore's mind about transporting Willard and the PBR to the river, but from the map there is a Viet Cong-held village at the mouth of the river and Kilgore decides to capture the village. His men advise him that it's "Charlie's point" and heavily fortified. Dismissing this concern with the explanation that "Charlie don't surf!," Kilgore orders his men to saddle up in the morning to capture the town and the beach.

Riding high above the coast in a fleet of Hueys accompanied by OH-6As, Kilgore launches his attack on the beach. The scene, famous for its use of Richard Wagner's "Ride of the Valkyries," ends with the soldiers surfing the barely-secured beach amidst skirmishes between infantry and VC. After helicopters swoop over the village and demolish all visible signs of resistance, a giant napalm strike in the nearby jungle dramatically marks the climax of the battle. Kilgore exults to Willard, "I love the smell of napalm in the morning... The smell, you know that gasoline smell... Smells like, victory" as he recalls a battle in which a hill was bombarded with napalm for over twelve hours.

The lighting and mood darken as the boat navigates upstream and Willard's silent obsession with Kurtz deepens. Incidents on the journey include a run-in with a tiger while Willard and Chef search for mangoes. The boat continues up river and the crew watches a USO show featuring Playboy Bunnies and a centerfold that degenerates into chaos.

Shortly after the Playmate performance, Phillips spots a sampan and orders an inspection over the objections of Willard. Initially reluctant to board the boat, Chef impatiently searches it; a young woman on the boat makes a sudden movement towards a barrel, prompting Clean to open fire and kill nearly everyone on the sampan. As the woman lies dying, Chef discovers that the barrel contains the woman's pet puppy. Phillips insists on taking the woman to receive medical attention; however, Willard ends the debate by shooting her, calmly stating, "I told you not to stop," further alienating himself from the PBR's crew.

Act II

The boat moves up river to the American outpost at the Do Long bridge, the last U.S. Army outpost on the river, passing wreckage of a downed Huey helicopter and a B-52D Stratofortress. The boat arrives during a North Vietnamese attack on the bridge, which is under constant construction. Upon arrival, Willard receives the last piece of the dossier from a lieutenant named Carlson, along with mail for the boat crewmen. Willard goes ashore with Lance, who has taken LSD, and they make their way through the trenches where they encounter many panicked, leaderless soldiers. Realizing the situation has devolved into chaos, Willard and Lance return to the boat. The chief tries to convince Willard not to continue on with his mission. In response, Willard snaps at Phillips to continue upriver. As the boat departs, the NVA launch an artillery strike that destroys the bridge.

The next day, Willard learns from the information he received at Do Lung that an Army Captain named Colby was sent to find Kurtz a few months prior to Willard's assignment and is now missing. While the crew is busy reading mail, Lance pops open a purple smoke grenade, catching the attention of an unseen enemy hiding in the trees by the river, and prompting an attack on the boat. Clean is killed as he listens to an audio tape from his mother. The chief, who had a close relationship with Clean, becomes increasingly hostile to Willard.

Later, Montagnard villagers begin shooting arrows at the boat as it approaches the camp. The crew opens fire until the chief is hit by a spear. Willard attempts to assist the mortally wounded Phillips, who tries to kill Willard by pulling him onto the spear tip protruding from his chest. Willard grapples with Phillips until the man finally dies. Afterwards, Willard confides in Chef and Lance about his mission, and the two surviving crew of the boat reluctantly agree to continue their journey upriver as they are now in Cambodia. As they draw closer, they see the coastline is littered with dead bodies.

After arriving at Kurtz' outpost, Willard leaves Chef behind with orders to call in an airstrike on the village if he does not return and takes Johnson with him to the village. They are met by a manic freelance photographer (Dennis Hopper), who explains that Kurtz's greatness and philosophical skills inspire his people to follow him. As they go into the village, there are bodies that are ignored by the villagers, as well as severed heads scattered about the nearby Buddhist temple which serves as Kurtz's living quarters. Willard also encounters the missing Captain Colby, who is in a nearly catatonic state.

Willard is bound and brought before Kurtz in the darkened temple. Kurtz lectures him on his theories of war, humanity, and civilization. Kurtz explains his motives and philosophy in a haunting monologue in which he praises the ruthlessness of the Viet Cong which he witnessed firsthand after one of his own humanitarian missions. He recalls the incident as leaving him traumatised but also giving him a new and deeper understanding of the complexities of his enemy and the level to which the US would have to commit in order to prevail.

The scene changes to Chef attempting to call in the airstrike on the village as ordered by Willard. Chef is attacked before the call is completed, and the scene cuts to Willard bound to a post outside in the pouring rain. Kurtz walks up to him and drops Chef's severed head into his lap.

Sometime later, a villager releases Willard's bonds and gives him a machete. Willard enters Kurtz's chamber as Kurtz is making a recording, and attacks him with the machete. This entire sequence is set to "The End" by The Doors and juxtaposed with a ceremonial slaughtering of a water buffalo.

Lying bloody and dying on the ground, Kurtz whispers "The horror... the horror..." before expiring. Willard descends the stairs from Kurtz' chamber and drops his weapon. The villagers do so as well. Willard walks through the now-silent crowd of natives and takes the last surviving crewperson, the near-catatonic Lance, by the hand. With his mission accomplished, Willard leads Johnson to the PBR, and the two of them sail away downriver as Kurtz's final words echo and the scene fades to black. In some but not all prints of the film, the closing credits play over footage of Kurtz' temple-base exploding; after the film's original general release Coppola replaced this footage with a plain black screen because some viewers interpreted it as an air strike called in by Willard, which Coppola did not intend.

Cast

- Martin Sheen as Captain Benjamin L. Willard. Willard is a veteran officer who has been serving in Vietnam for three years. He wears the insignia of the elite 173rd Airborne Brigade, and it is implied Willard had done missions for MACV-SOG and the CIA. An attempt to re-integrate into home-front society had apparently failed prior to the time at which the movie is set, and so he returned to the war-torn jungles of Vietnam, where he seemed to feel more at home.
- Marlon Brando as Colonel Walter E. Kurtz, a highly decorated American Army Special Forces officer who goes renegade. He runs his own operations out of Cambodia and is feared by the US military as much as the Vietnamese.
- Frederic Forrest as Engineman 3rd Class Jay "Chef" Hicks, a tightly-wound former chef from New Orleans who is horrified by his surroundings.
- Sam Bottoms as Gunner's Mate 3rd Class Lance B. Johnson, a former professional surfer from California who spends the majority of the journey on a drug binge.
- Laurence Fishburne (as "Larry Fishburne") as Gunner's Mate 3rd Class Tyrone "Mr. Clean" Miller, the 17 year-old cocky South Bronx-born crewmember. He resents the inward nature of Willard.
- Albert Hall as Chief Quartermaster George Phillips. The chief runs a tight ship and frequently clashes with Willard over authority. Has a father-son relationship with Clean.
- Robert Duvall as Lieutenant Colonel William "Bill" Kilgore, 1st Squadron, 9th Air Cavalry Regiment commander and surfing fanatic. Kilgore is a strong leader who loves his men dearly but has methods that appear out-of-tune with the setting of the war. His character is a composite of several characters including Colonel John B. Stockton, General James F. Hollingsworth (featured in *The General Goes Zapping Charlie Cong* by Nicholas Tomalin), George Patton IV, also a West Point officer who Robert Duvall knew and possibly Col. David Hackworth.
- Dennis Hopper as an American Photojournalist, a crazed photographer who intercuts poetry with obscene cynicism. Stranded in Kurtz's camp. Takes pictures from a camera that may or may not contain film. According to the DVD commentary of Redux, the journalist is supposed to be a real life photographer who went missing in Vietnam in 1966. Coppola stated that Hopper's character is supposed to be the real life journalist Sean Flynn years later; the real Flynn was also a character in Herr's Dispatches. The Hopper part was also based in part on the "harlequin" (patchwork) figure in Heart of Darkness that greets Marlow; Hopper repeats the harlequin's "the man's enlarged my mind" soliloquy.
- G.D. Spradlin as Lieutenant General Corman, military intelligence (G-2) an authoritarian officer who fears Kurtz and wants him removed.

- Jerry Ziesmer as a mysterious man in civilian attire who sits in on Willard's initial briefing, is the only one calm enough to eat during the briefing, and whose only line in the movie is the famous "Terminate with extreme prejudice".
- Harrison Ford as Colonel Lucas, aide to Corman and general information specialist. Despite his rank, he often appears nervous and jittery regarding Kurtz and the mission.
- Scott Glenn as Captain Richard M. Colby, previously assigned Willard's current mission before he defected to Kurtz's private army and sent a message to his wife telling her to sell everything they owned (but he goes on to tell her to sell their children, as well).
- Bill Graham as Agent (announcer and in charge of Playmate's show)
- Cynthia Wood as Playmate of the Year
- Colleen Camp as Playmate, "Miss May"
- Linda Carpenter as Playmate, "Miss August"
- Christian Marquand as Hubert de Marais (redux version), the surrogate leader of the French residents and strong vocal opponent of American action.
- Aurore Clément as Roxanne Sarraut-de Marais (redux version), a widow and influential figure at the plantation.
- Roman Coppola as Francis de Marais (redux version)
- Francis Coppola himself has a cameo as a director filming beach combat. He shouts "Don't look at the camera, keep on fighting!" DP Vittorio Storaro plays the cameraman by Coppola's side.

Several actors who were, or later became, prominent stars have minor roles in the movie including Harrison Ford, G. D. Spradlin, Scott Glenn, and R. Lee Ermey. Fishburne was only fourteen years old when shooting began in March 1976, and he lied about his age in order to get cast in his role. *Apocalypse Now* took so long to finish that Fishburne was seventeen (the same age as his character) by the time of its release.

Adaptation

Although inspired by Joseph Conrad's *Heart of Darkness*, the film deviates extensively from its source material. The novella, based on Conrad's real experiences as a steam paddleboat captain in Africa, is set in the Congo Free State during the 19th century. Kurtz and Marlow (who is named Willard in the movie) both work for a Belgian trading company that brutally exploits its native African workers.

When Marlow arrives at Kurtz's outpost, he discovers that Kurtz has gone insane and is lording over a small tribe as a god. The novella ends with Kurtz dying on the trip back and the narrator musing about darkness of the human psyche: "the heart of an immense darkness."

In the novella, Marlow is the pilot of a river boat sent to collect ivory from Kurtz's outpost, only gradually becoming infatuated with Kurtz. In fact, when he discovers Kurtz in terrible health, Marlow makes an effort to bring him home safely. In the movie, Willard is an assassin dispatched to kill Kurtz. Nevertheless, the depiction of Kurtz as a god-like leader of a tribe of natives and his malarial fever,

Kurtz's written exclamation "Exterminate the brutes!" (which appears in the film as "Drop the bomb. Exterminate them All!") and his final lines "The horror! The horror!" are taken from Conrad's novella.

Coppola argues that many episodes in the film—the spear and arrow attack on the boat, for example—respect the spirit of the novella and in particular its critique of the concepts of civilization and progress. Other episodes adapted by Coppola, the Playboy bunnies (Sirens) exit, the lost souls, "taking me home" attempting to reach the boat and Kurtz' tribe of (white-faced) natives parting the canoes (gates of Hell) for Willard, (with Chef and Lance) to enter the camp are likened to Virgil and "The Inferno" (Divine Comedy) by Dante. While Coppola replaced European colonialism with American interventionism, the message of Conrad's book is still clear.

Coppola's interpretation of the iconic Kurtz character is often speculated to have been modeled after Tony Poe, a highly-decorated Vietnam-era Paramilitary Officer from the CIA's Special Activities Division. Poe's actions in Vietnam and in the 'Secret War' in neighbouring Laos, in particular his highly unorthodox and often savage methods of waging war show many similarities to those of the fictional Kurtz; for example, Poe was known to drop severed heads into enemy-controlled villages as a form of psychological warfare and use human ears to record the number of enemies his indigenous troops had killed. He would send these ears back to his superiors as proof of the efficacy of his operations deep inside Laos. Coppola, however, denies that Poe was a primary influence and instead says the character was loosely based on Special Forces Colonel Robert Rheault, whose 1969 arrest over the murder of a suspected double agent Thai Khac Chuyen in Nha Trang generated substantial contemporary news coverage.

Usage of Poetry of T.S. Eliot

In the film, shortly before his death, Colonel Kurtz recites most of T.S. Eliot's poem *The Hollow Men*. Not only is Kurtz in the novel characterized as "hollow to the core", the poem is preceded in printed editions by the epigraph *"Mistah Kurtz - he dead"*, a quotation from Conrad's *Heart of Darkness* which was, itself, the inspiration for the film.

In addition, two books seen opened on Kurtz' desk in the film are *From Ritual to Romance* by Jessie Weston and *The Golden Bough* by Sir James Frazer, the two books that Eliot cited as the chief sources and inspiration for his poem *The Waste Land*.

Development

While working as an assistant for Francis Ford Coppola on *The Rain People*, George Lucas and Steven Spielberg encouraged their friend and filmmaker John Milius to write a Vietnam War film. Milius came up with the idea for adapting the plot of Joseph Conrad's *Heart of Darkness* to the Vietnam War setting. He had no desire to direct the film and felt that George Lucas was the right person for the job. However, filmmaker Carroll Ballard claims that *Apocalypse Now* was his idea in 1967 before Milius had written his screenplay. Ballard had a deal with producer Joel Landon and they tried to get the rights to Conrad's book but were unsuccessful. Lucas acquired the rights but failed to tell Ballard and Landon.

Screenplay

Coppola gave Milius $15,000 to write the screenplay with the promise of an additional $10,000 if it got made. Milius claims that he wrote the screenplay in 1969 and it was originally called *The Psychedelic Soldier*. He wanted to use Conrad's novel as "a sort of allegory. It would have been too simple to have followed the book completely". He based the character of Willard and some of Kurtz on a friend of his, Fred Rexer, who had experienced, first-hand, the scene related by Marlon Brando's character where the arms of villagers are hacked off by the Viet Cong. At one point, Coppola told Milius, "write every scene you ever wanted to go into that movie", and he wrote ten drafts, amounting to over a thousand pages. Milius changed the film's title to *Apocalypse Now* after being inspired by a button badge popular with hippies during the 1960s that said "Nirvana Now". He was also influenced by an article written by Michael Herr entitled, "The Battle for Khe Sanh", which referred to drugs, rock 'n' roll, and people calling airstrikes down on themselves.

Pre-production

Coppola was drawn to Milius' script, which he described as "a comedy and a terrifying psychological horror story". George Lucas was originally interested in directing and planned to shoot it after making *THX 1138* with principal photography to start in 1971. He planned to shoot the film in the rice fields between Stockton and Sacramento, California. His friend and producer Gary Kurtz traveled to the Philippines, scouting suitable locations. They intended to shoot the film on a $2 million budget, documentary style, using 16 mm cameras, and real soldiers. However, Lucas became involved with *American Graffiti* and this delayed the production of *Apocalypse Now*. In the spring of 1974, Coppola discussed with friends and co-producers Fred Roos and Gary Frederickson the idea of producing the film.

While making *The Godfather Part II*, Coppola asked Lucas and then Milius to direct *Apocalypse Now*, but both men were involved with other projects, in Lucas' case, he got the go-ahead to make his pet project, *Star Wars*, and declined the offer to direct *Apocalypse Now*. Coppola was determined to make the film and pressed ahead himself. He envisioned the film as a definitive statement on the nature of modern war, the difference between good and evil, and the impact of American society on the rest of the world. The director said that he wanted to take the audience "through an unprecedented experience of war and have them react as much as those who had gone through the war".

In 1975, while promoting *The Godfather Part II* in Australia, Coppola and his producers scouted possible locations for *Apocalypse Now* in Cairns in northern Queensland that had jungle resembling Vietnam. He decided to make his film in the Philippines for its access to American equipment and cheap labor. Production coordinator Fred Roos had already made two low-budget films there for Monte Hellman and had friends and contacts in the country. Coppola spent the last few months of 1975 revising Milius' script and negotiating with United Artists to secure financing for the production. According to Frederickson, the budget was estimated between $12–14 million. Coppola's American Zoetrope assembled $8 million from distributors outside the United States and $7.5 million from United Artists who assumed that the film would star Marlon Brando, Steve McQueen, and Gene Hackman. Frederickson went to the Philippines and had dinner with President Ferdinand Marcos to formalize support for the production and to allow them to use some of the country's military equipment.

Casting

Steve McQueen was Coppola's first choice to play Willard but the actor did not accept because he did not want to leave America for 17 weeks. Al Pacino was also offered the role but he too did not want to be away for that long period of time and was afraid of falling ill in the jungle as he had done in the Dominican Republic during the shooting of *The Godfather Part II*. Jack Nicholson, Robert Redford, and James Caan were approached to play either Kurtz or Willard. Coppola and Roos had been impressed by Martin Sheen's screen test for Michael in *The Godfather* and he became their top choice to play Willard but the actor had already accepted another project and Harvey Keitel was cast in the role based on his work in Martin Scorsese's *Mean Streets*. By early 1976, Coppola had persuaded Marlon Brando to play Kurtz for a then-unheard of fee - $3.5 million for a month's work on location in September 1976. Dennis Hopper was cast as a kind of Green Beret sidekick for Kurtz and when Coppola heard him talking nonstop on location, he remembered putting "the cameras and the Montagnard shirt on him, and we shot the scene where he greets them on the boat".

Principal photography

On March 1, 1976, Coppola and his family flew to Manila and rented a large house there for the five-month shoot. Sound and photographic equipment had been coming in from California on a regular basis since late 1975. Principal photography began three weeks later. Within a few days, Coppola was not happy with Harvey Keitel's take on Willard, saying that the actor "found it difficult to play him a passive onlooker". After viewing early footage, the director took a plane back to Los Angeles and replaced Keitel with Martin Sheen.

Typhoon Olga wrecked the sets at Iba and on May 26, 1976, production was closed down. Dean Tavoularis remembers that it "started raining harder and harder until finally it was literally *white* outside, and all the trees were bent at forty-five degrees". One part of the crew was stranded in a hotel and the others were in small houses that were immobilized by the storm. The Playboy Playmate set had been destroyed, ruining a month's shooting that had been scheduled. Most of the cast and crew went back to the United States for six to eight weeks. Tavoularis and his team stayed on to scout new locations and rebuild the Playmate set in a different place. Also, the production had bodyguards watching constantly at night and one day the entire payroll was stolen. According to Coppola's wife, Eleanor, the film was six weeks behind schedule and $2 million over budget.

Coppola flew back to the U.S. in June 1976. He read a book about Genghis Khan to get a better handle on the character of Kurtz. After filming commenced, Marlon Brando arrived in Manila very overweight and began working with Coppola to rewrite the ending. The director downplayed Brando's weight by dressing him in black, photographing only his face, and having another, taller actor double for him in an attempt to portray Kurtz as an almost mythical character.

In the days after Christmas 1976, Coppola viewed a rough assembly of the footage he had to date but still needed to improvise an ending. He returned to the Philippines in early 1977 and resumed filming. On March 5, 1977, Sheen had a heart attack and struggled for a quarter of a mile to reach help. He was back on the set on April 19. A major sequence in a French plantation cost hundreds of thousands of dollars but was cut from the final film. Rumors began to circulate that *Apocalypse Now* had several endings but Richard Beggs, who worked on the sound elements, said, "There were never *five* endings, but just the one, even if there were differently *edited* versions". These rumors came from Coppola departing frequently from the original screenplay. Coppola admitted that he had no ending because Brando was too fat to play the scenes as written in the original script. With the help of Dennis Jakob, Coppola decided that the ending could be "the classic myth of the murderer who gets up the river, kills the king, and then himself becomes the king — it's the Fisher King, from *The Golden Bough*".

A water buffalo was slaughtered with a machete for the climactic scene. The scene was inspired by a ritual performed by a local Ifugao tribe which Coppola had witnessed along with his wife (who filmed the ritual later shown in the documentary *Hearts of Darkness*) and film crew. Although this was an American production subject to American animal cruelty laws, scenes like this filmed in the Philippines were not policed or monitored, and the American Humane Association gave the film an "unacceptable" rating. Principal photography ended on May 21, 1977 and everyone headed home.

Post-production

In the summer of 1977, Coppola told Walter Murch that he had four months to assemble the sound. Murch realized that the script had been narrated but Coppola abandoned the idea during filming. Murch thought that there was a way to assemble the film without narration but it would take ten months and decided to give it another try. He put it back in, recording it all himself. By September, Coppola told his wife that he felt "there is only about a 20% chance [I] can pull the film off". He convinced United Artists executives to delay the premiere from May to October 1978. Author Michael Herr received a call from Zoetrope in January 1978 and was asked to work on the film's narration based on his well-received book about Vietnam, *Dispatches*. Herr said that the narration already written was "totally useless" and spent a year writing various narrations with Coppola giving him very definite guidelines.

Murch had problems trying to make a quadraphonic soundtrack for *Apocalypse Now* because sound libraries were devoid of any stereo recordings of any weapons and, specifically, weapons used in Vietnam. In addition, the sound material brought back from the Philippines was inadequate because the small location crew lacked time and resources sufficient to record jungle sounds and ambient noises.

Murch and his crew had to fabricate the mood of the jungle on the soundtrack. *Apocalypse Now* would feature innovative sound technique for movies as Murch insisted on recording the most up-to-date gunfire and employed a quintaphonic soundtrack with three channels of sound behind the movie screen and two channels of sound from behind the audience.

In May 1978, Coppola decided that it would not be possible to finish the film for a December release and postponed the opening until spring of 1979. He screened a "work in progress" for 900 people in April 1979 that was not well-received. That same year, he was invited to screen *Apocalypse Now* at the Cannes Film Festival. United Artists were not keen on showing an unfinished version in front of so many members of the press but Coppola remembered that *The Conversation* won the Palme d'Or and agreed to show *Apocalypse Now* at the festival less than a month before it began. The week prior to Cannes, Coppola arranged three sneak previews that each featured their own slightly different versions. He allowed critics to attend the screenings and believed that they would honor the embargo placed on reviews. On May 14, Rona Barrett reviewed the film on television and called it "a disappointing failure". At Cannes, Zoetrope technicians worked during the night before the screening to install additional speakers on the theater walls in order to achieve Murch's quintaphonic soundtrack. On August 15, 1979 *Apocalypse Now* was released in the U.S. in 15 theaters equipped to play the first Dolby Stereo 70 mm film with surround sound.

Other versions

Endings

At the time of its release, many rumors surrounded the ending of *Apocalypse Now*. Coppola stated an ending was written in haste in which Willard and Kurtz joined forces and repelled the air strike on the compound; however, Coppola never fully agreed with the two going out in apocalyptic intensity, preferring to end the film in a more encouraging manner.

When Coppola originally organized the ending of the movie, he had two choices. One involved Willard leading Lance by the hand as everyone in Kurtz's base throws down their weapons, and ends with images of Willard's boat pulling away from Kurtz's compound superimposed over the face of a stone idol which then fades into black. Another option showed an air strike being called and the base being blown to bits in a spectacular display, consequently killing everyone left at the base.

The original 1979 70 mm exclusive theatrical release ended with Willard's boat, the stone statue, then fade to black with no credits, save for '"Copyright 1979 Omni Zoetrope"' right after the film ends. This mirrors the lack of any opening titles and supposedly stems from Coppola's original intention to "tour" the film as one would a play: the credits would have appeared on printed programs provided before the screening began. For general release in 35mm, Coppola elected to show the credits superimposed over shots of Kurtz's base exploding. Rental prints circulated with this ending, and can be found in the hands of a few collectors. However, when Coppola heard that audiences interpreted this as an air strike called by Willard, Coppola pulled the film from its 35 mm run, and put credits on a black screen. In the DVD commentary, Coppola explains that the images of explosions had not been intended to be part of the story; they were intended to be seen as completely separate from the film. He had added them to the credits because he had captured the footage during the demolition of the sets (required by the Philippine government), which was filmed with multiple cameras fitted with different film stocks and lenses to capture the explosions at different speeds.

Because of the confusion over the misinterpreted ending, there are multiple slightly varying versions of the ending credits. Some TV screenings maintain the explosion footage at the end, others do not, and there are several other versions.

In the Redux Version, Willard silences the radio, and thus fails to stop the air strike on Kurtz's compound. Just before fading to black, Kurtz's last words "the horror" are echoed and there is a brief glimpse of helicopters and napalm.

Extended bootleg version

There is a longer 289 minute version which has never been officially released but circulates as a video bootleg, containing extra material not included in either the original theatrical release or the "redux" version.

Apocalypse Now Redux

Main article: Apocalypse Now Redux

In 2001, Coppola released *Apocalypse Now Redux* in cinemas and subsequently on DVD. This is an extended version that restores 49 minutes of scenes cut from the original film. Coppola has continued to circulate the original version as well: the two versions are packaged together in the *Complete Dossier* DVD, released on August 15, 2006.

The longest section of added footage in the *Redux* version is an anticolonialism chapter involving the de Marais family's rubber plantation, a holdover from the colonization of French Indochina, featuring Coppola's two sons Giancarlo and Roman as children of the family. These scenes were removed from the 1979 cut, which premiered at Cannes. In behind-the-scenes footage in *Hearts of Darkness*, Coppola expresses his anger, on the set, at the technical aspects of the shot scenes, the result of tight allocation of resources. At the time of the *Redux* version, it was possible to digitally enhance the footage to accomplish Coppola's vision. In the scenes, the French family patriarchs argue about the positive side of colonialism in Indochina and denounce the betrayal of the military men in the First Indochina War. Hubert de Marais argues that French politicians sacrificed entire battalions at Điện Biên Phủ, and tells Willard that the US created the Viet Cong (as the Viet Minh), to fend off Japanese invaders.

Other added material includes extra combat footage before Willard meets Kilgore, a humorous scene in which Willard's team steals Kilgore's surfboard (which sheds some light on the hunt for the mangoes), a follow-up scene to the dance of the *Playboy* playmates, in which Willard's team finds the playmates awaiting evacuation after their helicopter has run out of fuel, and a scene of Kurtz reading from a *Time* magazine article about the war, surrounded by Cambodian children.

There is a deleted scene entitled "Monkey Sampan" which was used as a way to represent the whole movie in a three minute scene. The scene shows Willard and the PBR crew suspiciously eyeing an approaching Sampan juxtaposed to Montagnard villagers joyfully singing "Light My Fire" by The Doors. As the Sampan gets closer Willard realizes there are monkeys on it and no helmsman. Finally just as the two boats pass, the wind turns the sail and exposes a naked dead civilian tied to the sail boom. His body is mutilated and looks as though the man was whipped. The singing stops. It is assumed the man was tortured by the Viet Cong. As they pass on by, Chief notes out loud "That's comin' from where we're going, Captain." The boat then slowly passes the giant tail of a shot down B-52 bomber. The scene is ominous and the noise of engines way up in the sky is heard. Coppola said that he made up for cutting this scene by having the PBR pass under an airplane tail in the final cut.

Reaction

Cannes screening

A three-hour version of *Apocalypse Now* was screened as a "work in progress" at the 1979 Cannes Film Festival and met with prolonged applause. At the subsequent press conference, Coppola criticized the media for attacking him and the production during their problems filming in the Philippines and uttered the famous quotes, "We had access to too much money, too much equipment, and little by little we went insane", and "My film is not about Vietnam, it *is* Vietnam". The filmmaker upset newspaper critic Rex Reed who reportedly stormed out of the conference. *Apocalypse Now* won the Palme d'Or for best film along with Volker Schlöndorff's *The Tin Drum* - a decision that was reportedly greeted with "some boos and jeers from the audience".

Box office

Apocalypse Now performed well at the box office when it opened in August 1979. The film initially opened in one theater in New York City, Toronto, and Hollywood, grossing USD $322,489 in the first five days. It ran exclusively in these three locations for four weeks before opening in an additional 12 theaters on October 3, 1979 and then several hundred the following week. The film grossed over $78 million domestically with a worldwide total of approximately $150 million.

The film was re-released on August 28, 1987 in six cities to capitalize on the success of *Platoon*, *Full Metal Jacket* and other Vietnam War movies. New 70mm prints were shown in Los Angeles, San Francisco, San Jose, Seattle, St. Louis, and Cincinnati — cities where the film did financially well in 1979. The film was given the same kind of release as the exclusive engagement in 1979 with no logo or credits and audiences were given a printed program.

Critical response

On the review aggregate website Rotten Tomatoes, *Apocalypse Now* has a 98% "Certified Fresh" rating. The Consensus is "Francis Ford Coppola's haunting, hallucinatory Vietnam war epic is cinema at its most audacious and visionary." In his original review, Roger Ebert wrote, "*Apocalypse Now* achieves greatness not by analyzing our 'experience in Vietnam', but by re-creating, in characters and images, something of that experience". In his review for the *Los Angeles Times*, Charles Champlin wrote, "as a noble use of the medium and as a tireless expression of national anguish, it towers over everything that has been attempted by an American filmmaker in a very long time".

Ebert added Coppola's film to his list of Great Movies, stating: "*Apocalypse Now* is the best Vietnam film, one of the greatest of all films, because it pushes beyond the others, into the dark places of the soul. It is not about war so much as about how war reveals truths we would be happy never to discover".

Other reviews were less positive, Frank Rich in *Time* said "while much of the footage is breathtaking, Apocalypse Now is emotionally obtuse and intellectually empty."

Legacy

Today, the film is widely regarded as a masterpiece of the New Hollywood era. It is on the American Film Institute's *100 Years... 100 Movies* list at number 28, but it dropped two spots to number 30 on their 10th anniversary list. Kilgore's quote "I love the smell of napalm in the morning" (written by Milius) was number 12 on the AFI's *100 Years... 100 Movie Quotes* list.

In 2002, *Sight and Sound* magazine polled several critics to name the best film of the last 25 years and *Apocalypse Now* was named number one. It was also listed as the second best war film by viewers on Channel 4's *100 Greatest War Films*, and ranked number 1 on Channel 4's *50 Films To See Before You Die*. In a 2004 poll of UK film fans, Blockbuster listed Kilgore's eulogy to napalm as the best movie speech. The helicopter attack to Ride of the Valkyries was chosen as the most memorable film scene ever by the *Empire* magazine.

In 2009, the London Film Critics' Circle voted *Apocalypse Now* the best movie of the last 30 years.

The film – particularly the helicopter attack scene – is referenced in many works of popular culture, including James Cameron's 2009 film *Avatar*.

Awards and honors

Wins

- Academy Award for Best Cinematography (Vittorio Storaro)
- Academy Award for Best Sound (Walter Murch, Mark Berger, Richard Beggs, Nathan Boxer)
- Cannes Film Festival: Palme d'Or
- Golden Globe Award for Best Director (Francis Ford Coppola)
- Golden Globe Award for Best Supporting Actor (Robert Duvall)
- Golden Globe Award for Best Original Score (Carmine Coppola and Francis Ford Coppola)
- National Society of Film Critics Award for Best Supporting Actor (Frederic Forrest)
- David di Donatello Award for Best Director, Foreign Film (Migliore Regista Straniero) (Francis Ford Coppola)
- American Movie Award for Best Supporting Actor (Robert Duvall)
- BAFTA Award for Best Direction (Francis Ford Coppola)
- BAFTA Award for Best Supporting Actor (Robert Duvall)

In 2000, *Apocalypse Now* was selected for preservation in the United States National Film Registry by the Library of Congress as being "culturally, historically, or aesthetically significant".

Nominations

- Academy Award for Best Picture (Francis Ford Coppola, Fred Roos, Gray Frederickson and Tom Sternberg)
- Academy Award for Best Supporting Actor (Robert Duvall)
- Academy Award for Best Art Direction — Set Decoration (Angelo P. Graham, George R. Nelson and Dean Tavoularis)
- Academy Award for Directing (Francis Ford Coppola)
- Academy Award for Film Editing (Lisa Fruchtman, Gerald B. Greenberg, Richard Marks and Walter Murch)
- Academy Award for Best Writing, Screenplay Based on Material from Another Medium (Francis Ford Coppola and John Milius)
- DGA Award for Outstanding Directorial Achievement in Motion Pictures (Francis Ford Coppola)
- WGA Award for Best Drama Written Directly for the Screen (John Milius and Francis Ford Coppola)
- Golden Globe Award for Best Motion Picture – Drama (Francis Ford Coppola, Fred Roos, Gray Frederickson and Tom Sternberg)
- Grammy Award for Best Original Score Written for a Motion Picture (Carmine Coppola and Francis Ford Coppola)
- César Award for Best Foreign Film (Meilleur film étranger) (Francis Ford Coppola)
- American Movie Award for Best Actor (Martin Sheen)
- BAFTA Award for Best Film Music (Carmine Coppola and Francis Ford Coppola)

- BAFTA Award for Best Actor (Martin Sheen)

American Film Institute recognition

- 1998 AFI's 100 Years... 100 Movies #28
- 2005 AFI's 100 Years... 100 Movie Quotes:
  - "I love the smell of napalm in the morning," #12
- 2007 AFI's 100 Years... 100 Movies (10th Anniversary Edition) #30

Star Marlon Brando was also named # 4 of the Top 25 American male screen legends.

Home video release aspect ratio issues

The first home video releases of *Apocalypse Now* were pan-and-scan versions of the original 35 mm Technovision anamorphic 2.35:1 print, and the closing credits, white on black background, were presented in compressed 1.33:1 full-frame format to allow all credit information to be seen on standard televisions. The first letterboxed appearance (on laserdisc on December 29, 1991) cropped the film to a 2:1 aspect ratio (conforming to the Univisium spec created by cinematographer Vittorio Storaro), featuring a small degree of pan-and-scan processing — notably in the opening shots in Willard's hotel room, featuring a composite montage — at the insistence of Coppola and Storaro. The end credits, from a videotape source rather than a film print, were still crushed for 1.33:1 and zoomed to fit the anamorphic video frame. All DVD releases have maintained this aspect ratio in anamorphic widescreen, but present the film without the end credits, which were treated as a separate feature. As a DVD extra, the footage of the explosion of the Kurtz compound was featured without text credits but included a commentary by director Coppola explaining the various endings based on how the film was screened. On the cover of the Redux DVD, Willard is erroneously listed as "Lieutenant Willard". It was announced that the upcoming Blu-ray release of *Apocalypse Now* will restore the film to its original 2.35:1 aspect ratio, making it the first home video release to display the film in its true aspect ratio.

Documentaries

Hearts of Darkness: A Filmmaker's Apocalypse (American Zoetrope/Cineplex-Odeon Films) (1991) Directed by Eleanor Coppola, George Hickenlooper & Fax Bahr

Apocalypse Now - The Complete Dossier DVD (Paramount Home Entertainment) (2006) Disc 2 Extras include:

The Post Production of Apocalypse Now: Documentary (four Featurettes covering the editing, music and sound of the film through Coppola and his team)

- A Million Feet of Film: The Editing of Apocalypse Now (18mins)
- The Music of Apocalypse Now (15mins)
- Heard Any Good Movies Lately? The Sound Design of Apocalypse Now (15mins)
- The Final Mix (3mins)

See also

- *Reflections in a Golden Eye*
- Cinema of the United States
- List of 1979 American films

References

Bibliography

- Adair, Gilbert (1981) *Vietnam on Film: From The Green Berets to Apocalypse Now*. Proteus. ISBN 09-06071-860
- Biskind, Peter (1999) *Easy Riders, Raging Bulls: How the Sex, Drugs and Rock-'n'-Roll Generation Saved Hollywood*. Simon and Schuster. ISBN 06-84857-081
- Coppola, Eleanor (1979) *Notes on the Making of Apocalypse Now*. Simon & Schuster. ISBN 0-87910-150-4
- Cowie, Peter (1990) *Coppola*. New York: Da Capo Press. ISBN 0306805987
- Cowie, Peter (2001) "The Apocalypse Now Book. *New York: Da Capo Press.ISBN 10-03068-104-68*
- Fraser, George MacDonald (1988) *The Hollywood History of the World: from One Million Years B.C. to Apocalypse Now*. Kobal Collection /Beech Tree Books. ISBN 06-88075-207
- French, Karl (1999) *Karl French on Apocalypse Now: A Bloomsbury Movie Guide*. Bloomsbury. ISBN 15-82340-145
- Milius, John & Coppola, Francis Ford (2001) *Apocalypse Now Redux: An Original Screenplay*. Talk Miramax Books/Hyperion. ISBN 07-86887-451
- Tosi, Umberto & Glaser, Milton. (1979) *Apocalypse Now* - Program distributed in connection with the opening of the film. United Artists

External links

- *Apocalypse Now* [1] at the Internet Movie Database
- *Apocalypse Now* [2] at Allmovie
- *Apocalypse Now* [3] at Box Office Mojo
- *Apocalypse Now* [4] at Rotten Tomatoes

Article Sources and Contributors

Indiana Jones *Source*: http://en.wikipedia.org/?oldid=390541724 *Contributors*: Petropoxy (Lithoderm Proxy)

Indiana Jones (franchise) *Source*: http://en.wikipedia.org/?oldid=389733713 *Contributors*:

Han Solo *Source*: http://en.wikipedia.org/?oldid=387634868 *Contributors*: Ironmanwarmachine115

Star Wars *Source*: http://en.wikipedia.org/?oldid=389558747 *Contributors*: TheRealFennShysa

Jack Ryan (Tom Clancy) *Source*: http://en.wikipedia.org/?oldid=390593445 *Contributors*: Moore103

Patriot Games (film) *Source*: http://en.wikipedia.org/?oldid=387203032 *Contributors*: Feyre

Clear and Present Danger (film) *Source*: http://en.wikipedia.org/?oldid=389936346 *Contributors*: 1 anonymous edits

Rick Deckard *Source*: http://en.wikipedia.org/?oldid=380217043 *Contributors*: AbramTerger

Blade Runner *Source*: http://en.wikipedia.org/?oldid=390661617 *Contributors*: Koavf

Richard Kimble *Source*: http://en.wikipedia.org/?oldid=369839738 *Contributors*: Dwanyewest

The Fugitive (1993 film) *Source*: http://en.wikipedia.org/?oldid=388575757 *Contributors*: RepublicanJacobite

American Graffiti *Source*: http://en.wikipedia.org/?oldid=386327136 *Contributors*: J 1982

Apocalypse Now *Source*: http://en.wikipedia.org/?oldid=389960947 *Contributors*:

Image Sources, Licenses and Contributors

Image:Indiana Jones Stunt Spectacular.jpg *Source*: http://bibliocm.bibliolabs.com/mwAnon/index.php?title=File:Indiana_Jones_Stunt_Spectacular.jpg *License*: Creative Commons Attribution-Sharealike 2.5 *Contributors*: Original uploader was Cybjorg at en.wikipedia

Image:Star Wars Logo.svg *Source*: http://bibliocm.bibliolabs.com/mwAnon/index.php?title=File:Star_Wars_Logo.svg *License*: Trademarked *Contributors*: User:KAMiKAZOW

Image:George Lucas.jpg *Source*: http://bibliocm.bibliolabs.com/mwAnon/index.php?title=File:George_Lucas.jpg *License*: Creative Commons Attribution 2.0 *Contributors*: Joi Ito from Inbamura, Japan

Image:StarToursEntrance96 wb.jpg *Source*: http://bibliocm.bibliolabs.com/mwAnon/index.php?title=File:StarToursEntrance96_wb.jpg *License*: Creative Commons Attribution-Sharealike 2.5 *Contributors*: Amineshaker, Electron, Elf, Gdgourou, Infrogmation

File:Bradbury Hotel.jpg *Source*: http://bibliocm.bibliolabs.com/mwAnon/index.php?title=File:Bradbury_Hotel.jpg *License*: Creative Commons Attribution 2.0 *Contributors*: Luke Jones

File:Bradbury Building, interior, ironwork.jpg *Source*: http://bibliocm.bibliolabs.com/mwAnon/index.php?title=File:Bradbury_Building,_interior,_ironwork.jpg *License*: Creative Commons Attribution 2.0 *Contributors*: Luke Jones

CPSIA information can be obtained
at www.ICGtesting.com
Printed in the USA
LVHW061044221220
674871LV00023B/250

9 781241 146429